MW00978471

Worship Heart Cries:

PERSONAL PREPARATION

FOR

CORPORATE WORSHIP

Ed Steele

Copyright © 2013 Ed Steele
All rights reserved.

ISBN: 1482719959
ISBN 13: 9781482719956

Library of Congress Control Number: 2013909703
CreateSpace Independent Publishing Platform
North Charleston, South Carolina

Contents

To Kathy:
an example of an obedient child of the Father
and loving wife reflecting a deep hunger
to understand and apply God's Word,
whose depth of relationship with Christ
has ever been an inspiration and encouragement to
me and our children, Kristi and David.

Introduction: Why this book was written

After teaching about worship for twenty years in Latin America as a missionary and over ten years in Seminary, I am more convinced than ever that there is a greater desire now to worship God than I have seen in years past. As great as the desire is, there seems to be more confusion as to what biblical worship is and even more confusion about what it looks like when we do it. Worship has been confused with buildings, clothing, music, and a host of other things.

I have well over 100 hundred books on worship and worship related topics in my personal library in my office and more seem to be published every week. With all this information about worship, one would think that there would be less confusion rather than more. If information alone could transform our worship, then we should have long since seen a revolution in our church services. But information is only part of the solution. Learning how to apply what we know may be the biggest challenge we face.

One of the key issues is not so much the amount of content available about worship, but how to worship. Over the years I have asked scores of groups how they knew that they had had a worship experience and the answers have been literally all over the map. If we are not sure what biblical worship is, we certainly will never know if we are following what Scripture teaches. More than likely, we will be basing our judgment of the comparison of others, other groups, or even just our on feelings to measure our worship. My sincere desire is to help push back all the preconceived notions and give some practical helps as we gather together for corporate worship. There are a multitude of resources available for personal spiritual growth and I would encourage their use, however the focus of this text is personal preparation for corporate worship.

When we gather as the Body of Christ we center our focus on Him, the Author and Perfecter of our faith and we do so *as the Body of Christ,* not just as individuals. Many look for what may be happening on the platform to determine their worship experience, but I believe one of the keys that has been missing is what is *not* happening in the pew. Blame is placed so easily on the preacher, the music, and so many other issues, without having examined to see if the Bride of Christ is ready to meet her groom. Regardless of who may be on the platform, only God's Spirit can transform those moments together into what may be called "worship," and there are some definite things that the Body must do so that worship may occur. What are they? That's the heart of this book.

I. Foundational Understandings Four Bases Authority

Introduction:

For the past several years my wife and I have lived in the New Orleans area, and besides the yearly hurricane watches, etc., I have learned something interesting about any building, house, even backyard patios constructed in the area: unless there are columns underneath, the foundation will crack or sink because the ground is unstable. This fact underscores an important fact for all of life: we must always build on secure foundations. So, before any discussion on worship and worship practices, it is imperative that we lay down some "support columns" on which we intend to build.

For the basis of this discussion, I would like to borrow from Ralph Neighbour's *Survival Kit for New Believers*, [Convention Press, 1981]. I have found it to be a great resource not only for followup for new believers, but foundational for this discussion.

There are four foundations from which we base our decisions: the *Word of God, History and Tradition, Human Intellect, or Reason, and Personal Experience.* Many of the arguments and debates over worship could have been put in perspective if only the parties involved had realized the truths found in understanding from what foundation we base our opinion.

The Word of God

Scripture, God's love letter and guide for living is the supreme authority for the believer. All that we think, do and feel is subject to the question: "Is this consistent with the teachings of the Word of God?" It would seem on the surface that if "its in the Book, that settles it." However, as many have found there are those who take the Bible and say things that are almost bizarre. For this reason, as we look in God's Word it is important that we remember some basics of interpretation. First there is the *Principle of Context.* We must first understand what the passage meant to the people to whom it was written, what the historical context was. A need to understand the passage in its original language as best is possible is a must. For example, there were several words that are translated in English as "love" in the Bible. Only by studying these can one determine which Greek word for love was being used. [There are many helpful tools for this and will be listed in the appendix at the end of the book.] We also need to look at the passage in light of the context of the book in which it was written as well as other related passages in Scripture.

This leads us to the next principle, the *Principle of Consistency.* The teachings of Scripture do not contradict each other. A helpful note is to remember that just because Scripture mentions something, it does not mean that it is teaching that as a principle. For example, the Bible mentions that Judas hung himself, but that does not mean that we need to go out and do the same. We need to look at the whole of Scripture to see what is being said and see if what we are understanding is consistent with the other related passages. There are untold dangers of just looking at verses without looking at the context or consistency.

That being said, the supreme authority, or basis of belief must be God's Word, His gift to us to teach us His ways and to lead us to an intimate relationship with Himself through His Son. In the case of a tie between feelings or experience, our logic and reasoning or our traditions and history, Scripture is the final and ultimate authority.

History and Tradition

History and tradition are good; they can keep us from having to "re-invent the wheel" every time we do something. It has been said that those who forget their history tend to repeat it, and that can be readily proven throughout history. History is a great teacher and traditions can link us with the past and give us an appreciation for things that are much bigger than our short span of years. Recently on a mission trip teaching in Havana, Cuba, I was able to visit the old fortress of *La Cabaña* and the firing of the cannon at 9:00 pm. For over the past 400 years, every evening at 9:00 pm, a cannon has been fired to announce the closing of the mouth of the bay. Even though now it is a re-enactment and tourist attraction, none the less as you listen to the soldiers dressed in the old Spanish costumes with their muskets and hear the sound of the steps across the stone pavement, you can close your eyes and imagine what it must have been like hundreds of years ago. My understanding has grown, and my identity with the past is strengthened because of my participation in it.

However, when activities are done without proper understanding of the purpose of the activity, problems can occur. I remember the story of the newlyweds and their first days of cooking supper. The husband noticed that his new bride dutifully cut off a considerable section of a ham they had purchased and set it aside, rather than cook the entire piece. When he asked her why she did it, she only replied, "that's the way Mama always cooked ham." So the next time they were at the mother-in-law's house the young husband asked his wife's mother about the ham. "Why do you always cut off one section of the ham before you cook it?" "Oh, that's simple," she replied, "I just don't have any pans big enough to cook it in." If we are not careful, we can be repeating things that at one time had significance, but the reasons for doing them can be lost over time and we follow practices that may or may not have justification.

Here's another illustration, perhaps a little closer to the subject. During the semester I ask each new class if they know why we generally have our worship services at about 11:00 am on Sundays. Each semester there are those who had never even considered the question and knew nothing of the rural roots of our faith and the fact that in the early days of our country many of the believers in the South were farmers and still had to get some chores done before they left for church. So, by the time they got things together, it was close to noon. By the way, because of this they generally brought a meal and shared it together for a "dinner on the ground." No where in Scripture is an exact hour given that we must meet for worship. The disciples met on the "first day of the week," but no specific hour was given. Since that is so, there is nothing sacred about that specific hour and churches should have the liberty to set the hour of worship at a time when it is most convenient for that congregation.

When we were serving as missionaries in Panama, I remember a specific church that had their Sunday morning worship service at 7:30 am due the fact they had a tin roof, no air conditioning or fans, and many of the members had to work on Sunday afternoon. The cooler morning hour helped with the brutal tropical heat and it set the course for the day in service to the Lord. History and tradition can be advisors, they can provide direction when we are not sure of the way, but only when they do not take precedence over Scripture. If Scripture doesn't prohibit, there can be flexibility.

Human Intellect

The gift of reason and the ability to draw conclusions is one of the most powerful tools given to men by God. God expects us to use wisely what He has provided for us. Great men of old developed the gift of reason given by God to help us understand the universe around us. Mathematics, physics, philosophy, science are means by which men and women have expressed their understanding of God's creation and laws, even when they failed to realize it was His doing. Christians should not be ashamed, or embarrassed in studying these subjects for fear that they will discover something that will destroy their faith. New discoveries

7

simply scratch the surface of the limitless knowledge of God and His creation. The field of Christian apologetics can greatly enhance our ability to deal with these issues.

All truth is God's truth. We do not discover anything that He did not know beforehand, and our "discovery" is just a way of describing what we see. However, as great as reason and logic are, we must never forget that our logic does have tainted roots, that we have "clay feet," and that we all belong to Adam's race. The story is told of the researcher who was studying fleas. He had his "control" flea and his group of "experimental" fleas. He told both groups to jump and recorded the results. Then he took tweezers and removed two legs from one of the experimental flea and repeated the command to jump. The flea jumped as before, only not quite as far. He then repeated the experiment after taking two more legs from the flea. After the command to jump, the flea obliged by the jumping, but it was even less than the previous one. After recording his findings, he removed the final two legs from the flea and instructed it to jump. The flea did not move, only laid there motionless. As the researcher was drawing his conclusions he wrote the following: "When you remove all the legs from a flea, he cannot hear one thing!" We may laugh at the twisted logic, but it does illustrate that our conclusions are not always without error. Only God can see the whole picture and how it works for His purpose, so we must depend on God's Word as the ultimate authority and not just our own reasoning ability.

Personal Experience

God grants us life and choices from which we have a myriad of experiences. Many of these become the basis for protective action, like the young man who picked up a hot dish without a pot holder. I can guarantee that he probably didn't do that again. Verbal instructions are one thing; burned fingers are another, and pot holders can become an instant friend. Life's experiences aren't always negative. My salvation experience, getting married, the birth of our children, seeing those with whom one has worked grow in the Lord and lead others to Christ are all amazing personal experiences and experiences that I cherish and refer to often.

We link our feelings to our faith through personal experiences. As a youth in Oklahoma, there was no place like the camp at Falls Creek in the Arbuckle mountains in the summer. The late '60's were filled with protests and demonstrations, but at Falls Creek thousands of students gathered week after week to study the Bible, worship together, and fellowship with one another. The first time I heard the 200+ voice choir, a 50 piece band and 5000 other students singing praise to God, I was completely overwhelmed. Surely heaven was opened up and the angels themselves were joining the crowds. It was an experience that was life changing for me. I know I am not alone, for many sense deep emotions as we worship, whether inspired by the music, the architecture, the sermon or other things.

As worship becomes more central to our experience, a myriad of experiences in response to worship will follow. Feelings are a part of our human makeup, and God created us that way. A person should not think himself or herself more spiritual if brought to tears during worship as compared to someone else who was not, or the other way around. Comparison with others is not the basis of judgment and we are not the judges. But we must remember that our sincerity and feelings may be wrong. We do not base our faith on feelings, but on God's Word. It is by "grace we are saved, through faith, and that not of ourselves, it is a gift of God" (Eph. 2:-8). Bob Kauflin tells the story of a visitor to some missionaries in Africa who were very moved by the music they heard. When asked what they were singing the missionary said "If you boil the water, you won't get dysentery."[1] Our emotions and feelings are a tricky slope and we must be very careful not to use them as a measure of our spiritual depth or maturity. As Scripture says, "the heart is deceitful above all things..." (Jeremiah 17:9). Only God's Word can link us with the true reality of God's wisdom and truth, regardless of how we might "feel." We must live by faith, not by feelings.

On occasions, I have heard some say that they didn't "feel" like worshiping, or that they didn't "feel" as though they had worshiped that day: the music was bad, the sermon boring, etc. It is important that we first have a biblical understanding of what worship is and is not. We will get more into that later in the book and there exists a plethora of excellent works on that subject. But, statements like "I didn't feel..." reveal than the basis of their understanding of worship is rooted more in feeling that in obedience and God's Word.

In worship, we must place our faith in Christ and His Word, regardless of "how we might feel." Limiting our worship experience to our feelings places us at the center of worship as the final judge. But worship is not "about us, but about Christ." We surrender our will, our lives, our actions, even our feelings to Him, regardless how we feel. It is an act of will. Many times our emotions will "catch up" with our will, but they are not necessary for us to worship. We must live in obedience. Consider yourself driving down the highway and the speed limit is 70 mph, and you are traveling between 69-70 mph. You are being "obedient" whether you "feel" that way or not. I also am painfully aware of times that I had been listening to some worship songs, but needing to get to the destination in a hurry resulting in going past the set legal speed limit on the freeway. Was what I was doing "worshiping," when I was really in direct disobedience to the laws of the road? There may be a varied set of opinions on that subject, but personally, I think not. I was definitely having an emotional response to the music being played, but worship cannot happen if we are not in obedience to what God demands. If this causes some doubts on your part, that is fine. Hang in there, keep reading and we'll keep on asking the Lord for discernment to help us along.

Personal experiences can also be misused as the basis of faith. Let's say that during a worship service one day that we jumped up came down and did the splits. Immediately afterwards, we felt a tremendous "feeling" that we interpreted as "worship." The next thing we did was to share that experience with the whole church and tell them, "If you want a deeper experience with God, you must jump up and do the splits! I have done it and it was so wonderful!" I have no doubt that before long there would be a host of others following that example. The only problem is Scripture does not teach us that jumping up and doing the splits is the basis for growth in

Christ. If Satan cannot keep us from worshiping Christ, he will push us past the biblical guidelines so that our basis is not in God's Word, but in our personal experience. I realize that the example is silly at best, but the truth there remains: Once our worship is based in personal experience rather than His Word, Satan has rendered our worship as fruitless.

So let's review: history and tradition are wonderful parts of our lives that help us avoid remaking the same mistakes and help up identify with His works and saints of the past. God has given us logic and reason as a gift to help us draw conclusions and live with understanding of that which is around us. Personal experiences and feelings are important, they help us link our faith to our daily lives, but nothing, not history, tradition, logic, human intellect, or personal experience can supersede the ultimate authority over our lives, which is the Word of God! It is always good to go back and see what the basis of our belief or authority is as we study about worship. When a question arises, ask yourself, "On what am I basing this belief, Scripture, history and tradition, human reason or logic, or personal experience?"

Working Definitions

A working definition of worship is necessary to continue. Almost every book on worship begins this way and virtually everyone is different, although they do have similar facets or qualities. Without some kind of boundaries, we are left to our own devices and ideas; working definitions can help limit the playing field and narrow our focus. For the purposes of this study, worship will be understood to mean *"that obedient response we give to God as we understand His nature and character.*" I am not demeaning heavy theological discussions, only wanting to use this as a point of departure. As our understanding of who God is and what He has done grows and our knowledge about what Scripture teaches about worship deepens, the definition will expand and take on more meanings and no doubt, grow in length.

II. Biblical Backgrounds

The Importance of Worship: Old Testament

Worship is central to the Scriptures from the beginning to the end. Worship is central to understanding the Old Testament. Man and woman were created by God for fellowship with Him and each other. Since we live in a post-Eden world, we cannot know what it must have been like to walk and talk with God without any hindrances. But for those who have a saving faith and knowledge of the Lord Christ, that unhindered walk will be part of what heaven is like. Whatever that walk was, it must have been unhindered worship as well. There are a number of wonderful texts that trace worship in detail, but our purposes here allow me to just highlight a few.

Consider the first sacrifices offered to God: those of Cain and Abel in Genesis 4. One was accepted and one was not. Since this predates any of the Jewish sacrificial system, one must look deeper than the fact that one of the offerings was with blood and the other wasn't. Timothy Pierce observes that Abel gave of his firstborn, while Cain just gave of the land's produce, implying a lack of intentionality. Worship had not been

15

commanded, but grew out of the relationship with God in the garden. Wrong worship led to tragic outcomes.[2] Worship continues to be central to the message.

Noah offered God a sacrifice upon leaving the ark. This act of worship was pleasing and came with a promise: "The LORD smelled the pleasing aroma and said in his heart: 'Never again will I curse the ground because of man, even though every inclination of his heart is evil from childhood. And never again will I destroy all living creatures, as I have done'" (Genesis 8:21).[3]

When Abraham arrives near Bethel in Canaan, God promises the land to him for his offspring, to which Abraham responds with building an altar (Genesis 12:7-9) and calling on the name of the Lord. He did this again when he moved to Mamre at Hebron (Genesis 13:18). When God promises him that he would be the father of a great nation, he falls face down in worship (Genesis 17:3). Perhaps the most defining moment in Abraham's life was when he built the altar in obedience to the commandment of God on Mt. Moriah, and laid his son, Isaac down as the sacrifice. (Genesis 22:9-11). This portion of Scripture has rightly been the source of much study and sermons, and could easily be a book in its own right. However, let's focus on just a few of the details that relate to the passage and worship.

The choice of Isaac as the sacrifice tested Abraham's obedience. But additionally it was a call to sacrifice. In the midst of that scene, the grace of God provided the solution: a ram was provided by God. Worship still demands sacrifice today, as was illustrated in this example of worship.

Abraham's life was so full of examples of the worship of God that even his servant responded in worship when God provided a wife for him to take back for Isaac (Genesis 24:26). Isaac worships when God reveals Himself and renews the covenant (Genesis 26:24-25). Jacob sets up a sacred stone and poured oil on top of it as an act of worship when God promises to bring him back to the land of his father Isaac (Genesis 28:16-18), and then again once he resettles in the land of Canaan (Genesis 33:20). When Jacob returns to Bethel, the place where God had previously spoken to him before leaving Canaan, he builds another altar to God (Genesis 35:4-7). Two other times Jacob is mentioned as worshiping: as he reaches Beer Sheba on his way to reunite with Joseph in Egypt (Genesis 46:1) and just before he blesses Joseph's sons (Genesis 47:31). Gratitude was central to worship then and now.

The life of Moses is punctuated with times of worship. Of the most notable worship experiences are his first meeting with God through the burning bush (Genesis 3) and the giving of the law in Exodus 19 and 20. It is interesting to note that the people's first response to Moses' signs and announcement of deliverance is worship (Exodus 4:31). The repeated request from God to Pharaoh through Moses was to "let my people go, that they may worship me," (Here the word used for worship is sometimes translated, "serve" implying that serving God is a part of worship; see Exodus 5:1, 7:16, 8:1, 8:20, 9:1, 9:13, and 10:5). The Passover was instituted as a time of worship (Exodus 12). Along their journey to Canaan, God provided manna, yet on the seventh day there was none, so that the time might be spent in rest and worship (Exodus 16:23). The celebration of the Passover was a call to remember the mighty acts of God and foreshadows the greatest act of God to come through Christ's atoning death and resurrection. True worship must involve recalling the mighty acts of God and responding in praise and adoration.

When Jethro, Moses' father-in-law heard all that God had done, his response was worship (Ex. 18:11-12). When God renews covenant with the children of Israel at Sinai, He tells them in Exodus 19:5-6: "Now if you obey me fully and keep my covenant, then out of all nations you will be my treasured possession. Although the whole earth is mine, you will be for me a kingdom of priests and a holy nation." The very description of their calling was related to worship, that is, being a "kingdom of priests." As priest, they would bring God's Word to others and help them respond to God in obedience and worship.

Not only does the Old Testament contain numerous examples of worship, but the importance of worship is also highlighted in the Ten Commandments given to the people of Israel by God. The first four commands cover man's relationship with God, and the last six commands cover man's relationship with other people.

Examine the first section in Exodus 20:2-8:

> [2]"I am the LORD your God, who brought you out of Egypt, out of the land of slavery.
> [3]"You shall have no other gods before me.
> [4]"You shall not make for yourself an image in the form of anything in heaven above or
> on the earth beneath or in the waters below. [5]You shall not bow down to them or worship them; for I, the LORD your God, am a jealous God, punishing the children for the sin of the parents to the third and fourth generation of those

who hate me, [6] but showing love to a thousand generations of those who love me and keep my commandments.

[7]"You shall not misuse the name of the LORD your God, for the LORD will not hold anyone guiltless who misuses his name.

[8]"Remember the Sabbath day by keeping it holy.

God reveals Himself as the LORD, Yahweh, the covenant keeping God, all powerful and deliverer, and then explains how He desires that His creation relate to Him:

1. The worship of God alone is primary.
2. Nothing should be done that would undermine the relationship with God.
3. One must not mis-communicate Who God is or disrespect Who God is.
4. One must set aside time to maintain the relationship with God.

When God gave His "ten words," what did He consider as first and foremost? Worship. Almost immediately after giving the commandments in Exodus 20, the writer of Exodus begins to deal with the details of the establishment of worship in the tabernacle (Exodus 25-31 and 35-40). The book of Leviticus is the book of regulations about the sacrifices used in worship. Chapter 3-4 of Numbers deals with the division of the Levites, whose responsibilities were separate from the priesthood and dealt with the practical aspects of moving and setting up the Tabernacle for worship.

Another biblical example of worshiping something or someone besides God is given in Numbers 22-24. Balak fails to convince Balaam to curse Israel, however, he succeeds in getting some of the Israelites to sin sexually and worship the Moabite idols (Numbers 25:1-3). Worshiping other idols remained such an on-going problem that as the Israelites approached the border of Canaan, the Promised Land, God had to command them to destroy the idols of the nations they would conquer (Numbers 33:50-56).

Once in the land of promise the emphasis on worship continues. In the repeating of the Covenant at Horeb, God reminds them again and again how important it was to be obedient in following the instructions He had given for worship (Deuteronomy 4:15-24, 32-39, 5:6-14, 11:16, 17:1, 26:10-11). For example, the first act of the Israelites after crossing the Jordan was to celebrate the Passover, an act of worship (Joshua 5:10). At the end of Joshua's life after the land had been divided, the leader calls them again to "choose this day who you will worship" (Joshua 24:14-24).

The book of Judges is the account of failure of the people to keep their commitment to worship Jehovah alone, their being defeated by their enemies and the restoration by a leader. Time and time again the author underscores that the people would fall back into the worship of idols and then God would allow the enemies around them to conquer and persecute them because of their lack of obedience. Each "judge" was really just a military leader who would call the people back to worshiping Jehovah alone.

Samuel's parents worshiped as they dedicated their young son to the service of the Lord (1 Samuel 1:24). The sons of Eli the High Priest were totally corrupt in their worship practice

20

and took the ark of God into battle using it as a "good luck charm." God revealed to them that obedience to His commands were primary as the Hebrew army was defeated, they were killed and the ark was taken captive. He wanted them to not confuse the trappings of worship with the worship of God, Himself (I Samuel 4-6). Samuel clarified that worship was more than just following the rituals of sacrifice ("to obey is better than sacrifice") after Saul disobeyed God's direct command to kill all the Amalekites (1 Samuel 15:22-35).

The life of David was a life of worship. Whether fleeing from Saul, fighting his enemies, or rejoicing in his victories, David's life was one marked by the adoration of Jehovah. He was the author of over half of the Psalms, the hymnbook of the Bible. David is the warrior king who was the "sweet singer of Israel" and at the heart of his songs was the worship of Yahweh. It was no wonder that one of the first things he did after reuniting the 12 tribes was to bring the ark of God to Jerusalem. Entire books have been written just on his life and deeds, so no attempt here will be made to add more detail.

David was not the only king who focused on worship. The apex of the reign of Solomon is the completion of the temple of God and his downfall was his failure to keep worship primary in his life. In Proverbs he declares that the "fear of the Lord is the beginning of wisdom," (1:7) which is that reverential awe of God. In spite of all his wisdom, he allowed his many wives to influence his own worship and eventually to worship other gods. Solomon's disobedience in worship led the way for the division of the kingdom, which occurred as the fulfillment of prophecy against him during the beginning of the reign of his son, Rehoboam. In the divided kingdom, Rehoboam is left with only Judah and Benjamin over which he is to reign, the other ten tribes choose Jeroboam as their king. The sin of Jeroboam was the creation of a convenient alternative option for worship, calves of gold, strategically located in the country and administered by those who had no preparation or calling to the priesthood. Jeroboam knew that if the people were to return to worship the Lord in Jerusalem they would be united once again, for worship is a unifying force. Later during the reign of Ahab, Elijah, God's prophet, calls the nation to repent and return to worship and fire falls to consume an evening sacrifice, but the repentance did not last. Leader after leader of the northern kingdom followed the ways of Jeroboam in idolatry and eventually the nation is defeated by the Assyrians and carried off into exile. Prophet after prophet had warned the leaders and the people, but to no avail. The summary of the story is found in 2 Kings 17:7-13:

> All this took place because the Israelites had sinned against the LORD their God, who had brought them up out of Egypt from under the power of Pharaoh king of Egypt. They worshiped other gods and followed the practices of the nations the LORD had driven out before them, as well as the practices that the kings of Israel had introduced. The Israelites secretly did things against the LORD their God that were not right. From watchtower to fortified city they built themselves high places in all their towns. They set up sacred stones and Asherah poles on every high hill and under every spreading

tree. At every high place they burned incense, as the nations whom the LORD had driven out before them had done. They did wicked things that aroused the LORD's anger. They worshiped idols, though the LORD had said, "You shall not do this."

Judah, the smaller of the divided kingdom, experienced occasional times of spiritual refreshment, centering around a return to the worship of Jehovah God and many times expressing that fervor with the celebration of the Passover. Only when they centered their lives around the worship of God and obedience to His commands did they prosper. However, in the end, they suffered the same fate by the hands of the Babylonians because of their disobedience toward God and failure in worshiping Him alone (2 Kings 24:20).

Many of the major themes in the books of the Old Testament centered around the return to worship: Ezra, and Haggai and the rebuilding of the Temple; the celebration and worship at the completion of the rebuilding of the wall in Nehemiah. Isaiah's experience of worship (6:1-8) will be covered later, which not only set the course for his life, but serves as an example for us as well. Jeremiah wept for the coming destruction of Jerusalem because of their failure to repent and worship as God had commanded. Ezekiel's vision displayed how the people had strayed from God and the Spirit of God leaving the Temple. Daniel was cast in the lion's den for his commitment to worship. God used Hosea to show that Judah's idolatry was like adultery. Micah reminded the people that worship was more than ritual, but "To act justly and to love mercy and to walk humbly with your God (6:8). Habakkuk taught to worship God despite the difficult circumstances. Malachi condemned the people for their careless attitude toward worship.

God's command and instructions regarding worship were clear. Time and time again the people of God chose to rebel against this mandate and began worshiping other gods. God allowed the enemies around Israel to punish their disobedience and many times the Israelites would repent and God would bring help. The tragic cycle of disobedience, discipline, and deliverance was repeated over again. Worship was a central focus in the old covenant.

Isaiah 6: Descriptive or Prescriptive?

Using the example mentioned previously, Scripture mentions that Judas hung himself, but no one would say that Scripture is teaching us to do the same. This might explain in part the difference between a passage being descriptive, or describing an event and one being prescriptive, or prescribing a specific action. Good biblical interpretation must look at the context in which a passage was written to see what it meant to the ones to whom it was written. Many heresies and poor biblical understanding stem from failure to study the historical and cultural context of the passage.

Another important issue is knowing how to apply what is being taught. If our understanding of God's Word only reaches to the level of understanding content and never reaches to the level of application, we will most likely end up as the guardians of wonderful biblical stories that have little connection with our everyday life. Recall Paul's admonition to the Romans: "*For everything that was written in the past was written to teach us, so that through the endurance taught in the Scriptures and the encouragement they provide we might have hope*" (Rom. 15:4). When the apostle wrote this, he was concluding his amazing treatise to the believers in Rome. While it is true that much of what we read in Scripture is historical documentary of what has happened to God's people in the past, Paul encourages those in Rome to look for the larger lessons or principles that might be applied to daily life. As we look at these passages to learn the lessons they might be teaching, we must remember that since Scripture does not contradict itself, the manner in which we interpret a particular passage must be consistent with what is taught in other passages of related material. With this in mind, let's look again at Isaiah 6:

> [1]In the year that King Uzziah died, I saw the Lord, high and exalted, seated on a throne; and the train of his robe filled the temple. [2]Above him were seraphim, each with six wings: With two wings they covered their faces, with two they covered their feet, and with two they were flying. [3]And they were calling to one another:
>
> "Holy, holy, holy is the LORD Almighty; the whole earth is full of his glory."
>
> [4]At the sound of their voices the doorposts and thresholds shook and the temple was filled with smoke.
>
> [5] "Woe to me!" I cried. "I am ruined! For I am a man of unclean lips, and I live among a people

of unclean lips, and my eyes have seen the King, the LORD Almighty."

[6] Then one of the seraphim flew to me with a live coal in his hand, which he had taken with tongs from the altar. [7]With it he touched my mouth and said, "See, this has touched your lips; your guilt is taken away and your sin atoned for."

[8]Then I heard the voice of the Lord saying, "Whom shall I send? And who will go for us?"

And I said, "Here am I. Send me!"

[9]He said, "Go and tell this people:

"'Be ever hearing, but never understanding;
be ever seeing, but never perceiving.'
[10]Make the heart of this people calloused;
make their ears dull
and close their eyes.
Otherwise they might see with their eyes,
hear with their ears,
understand with their hearts,
and turn and be healed."

[11]Then I said, "For how long, Lord?"

And he answered:
"Until the cities lie ruined
and without inhabitant,
until the houses are left deserted
and the fields ruined and ravaged,
[12] until the LORD has sent everyone far away
and the land is utterly forsaken.

¹³And though a tenth remains in the land,
it will again be laid waste.
But as the terebinth and oak
leave stumps when they are cut down,
so the holy seed will be the stump in the land."
(NIV)

Surely it is clear that this is God's call on the prophet's life, and this calling would change his life forever. In this light, Isaiah's calling is descriptive in nature–it is a description of his calling, not a specific calling for us today. However, this passage has been used as a model for worship, and in this sense it is interpreted as being prescriptive; that is, more of a command than a simple description. Recently I have been thinking through this passage, and I would like to share my understanding. Of course, my interpretation is not the only understanding of this passage.

First and foremost, we must see how God used this experience in the life of the prophet to enable him to complete the enormous task that lay before him, a task that would literally shape his life from then on. Elements we see in Isaiah's experience include: First, God takes the initiative to reveal Himself to Isaiah, revealing His nature, character, majesty, and holiness. A principle from this idea is that as we come to worship, we must recognize God is already present in us, and He is among us as we gather to worship Him. We don't "invoke the presence of God," but recognize His presence and authority, His holiness, that He is Almighty, Creator and the Everlasting One.

After having seen a vision of the holiness of the Almighty, the prophet sees himself as sinful and living among a sinful people. The most obvious response to having seen the perfection of the character of God is to see the imperfection in our own character. As we understand more of "who" God is in worship, we recognize who we are: sinners without hope, unworthy, except for the saving grace of our Lord Jesus Christ. Another important point is that the prophet confesses not only his own sin, but the sin of those around him: the confession of corporate sin. The prayers of Nehemiah and Ezra also illustrate the principle of publically confessing the sins of the people (Neh. 1:5-11; Ezra 9:5-15).

The prophet's confession precedes God's forgiveness, as symbolized by the burning coal from the altar. In confession of sin we come to agreement with what God has said that sin is; it is more than just admission of guilt. To confess sin means that sin is seen as God sees it; to come in agreement with God over sin. For Isaiah, the coal on his lips would also symbolize that he would be one who would proclaim the oracles of God; his mouth was purified to speak forth God's words as a commissioning to begin his prophetic ministry, and that is certainly what followed. However, it can also be see that his sin had been pardoned: "See, this has touched your lips; your guilt is taken away and your sin atoned for" (v.6).

Cleansed and forgiven, the prophet becomes able to hear God's voice: "Then, I heard the voice of the Lord saying..." (v.8). The word, "then" implies that something occurred, and based on the first occurrence, a second event took place. Not until the prophet had seen the holiness of God, admitted his own helpless condition, confessed and received forgiveness did the events that follow occur. "Then" he was able to hear

God's voice. We really don't know if there were any other people around Isaiah at the time or if this was just a revelation to him alone, but we do know that it wasn't until "then" that he was able to hear God's voice. In our worship, there is a very real possibility that we fail to hear God's voice because we aren't really ready or able to do so.

Hearing the voice of God was not the culmination of Isaiah's experience. Notice that God's declaration was open ended: "Then I heard the voice of the Lord saying, 'Whom shall I send? And who will go for us?'"(v.8) God did not call Isaiah by name and tell him to go, He simply revealed the need in an open-ended question. Now able to hear God's voice, the prophet responded, "Here am I. Send me!" (v.8). God clarified the mission in the verses that follow, with a discouraging warning that few would pay attention to Isaiah's message from God. The experience with God would forever burn in the prophet's memory: God had spoken, I must respond. In this example of a worship experience it is important to recognize that worship was not completed by just seeing God, or seeing one's self, or confessing sin and being forgiven. Worship was not complete because Isaiah was able to hear God's voice. Worship *was* completed when the prophet responded to what God had said. Too often we stop short in our worship by being content to be overwhelmed by God's nature and character but not willing for Him to purify us so that we can hear His voice and respond in obedience to what He demands.

There is nothing in the passage that declares that every follower of God must have such a vision; it is descriptive. However, the question must also be asked, "What lessons might be learned from Isaiah's experience? What lessons might be learned that are consistent with the teachings of the rest of Scripture?" First, God does take the initiative. God took the initiative in the garden of Eden to seek out Adam and Eve. He took the initiative to call out Abraham. The bush was burning, at God's initiative, before Moses ever turned around to see it. God's plan for salvation was formed before the creation of the world, – surely it is understood that God does take the initiative.

Another principle is that God reveals Himself: "The heavens declare the glory of God" (Ps. 19:1). The myriad of miracles throughout Scripture reveal that God continually shows His nature and character. A third principle in this passage speaks to the need for confessing sin and receiving the forgiveness of sin. We know that "our ways are not His ways" (Is. 55:8), and that "all have sinned and come short of the glory of God" (Rom. 3:23). The acknowledgment of sin is part of confession, which is coming in agreement with God in how He views our sin. We also know from God's Word that "if we confess our sin, He is faithful and just to forgive us our sins and cleanse us from all unrighteousness" (1 John 1:9). Sin breaks our fellowship with God and refusal to confess sin destroys the bridge to bring us back to Him (Is. 59:1-2). God reveals Himself as we respond in obedience to Him: "Whoever has my commands and keeps them is the one who loves me. The one who loves me will be loved by my Father, and I too will love them and show myself to them" (John 14:21).

Although the Isaiah passage is not prescriptive in that we all must have heavenly visions before for we can worship God and that every occasion of our worship must mirror step by step what happened in Isaiah's life, there are some similarities that do occur in worship. Scripture is clear that we must approach

30

the Father with "clean hands and a pure heart" (Ps. 24:3-4). In Jesus' parable, it is the repentant tax collector, not the Pharisee whom God hears (Luke 18:13). In this sense, one can see the similarities to Isaiah's experience and identify personal experiences with his.

There are many other experiences of worship described in Scripture that do not follow the experience of the prophet Isaiah. Many of David's songs of praise and worship are expressions of gratitude and exaltation. For example, in Psalm 100 we are commanded to "enter His gates with thanksgiving and his courts with praise," that is, praising Him for who he is and thanking Him for what He has done. Mary's declaration in Luke 2 became a song of praise for the early church. Paul and Silas were worshiping by singing praises to God before the earthquake (Acts 16:25). All of these are wonderful expressions of worship that must also be taken into account.

So what, then? What difference does all this make in my life and worship and that of the church where I worship? I'm glad you asked. Here are a few things to keep in mind that I believe will aid in our worship and are lessons learned from Isaiah and other examples of worship in the Bible. First we must remember that God has always taken the initiative. The culmination of His initiative-taking is seen in His providing for our salvation through Jesus Christ. We must realize that it is "in Him" and "through Him" that we come "to Him." Secondly, we must come with "clean hands and pure hearts." When David was moving the ark of God to Jerusalem, he failed to follow the instructions of using only Levites carrying it on poles. God struck Uzzah dead as he tried to steady the ark on the cart when the oxen stumbled. All the praise and celebration that David had organized could not make up for his lack of obedience[3] (1 Sam. 6). In the same way, we must come in obedience to God if we are to worship biblically. In addition, we must come to worship in gratitude and praise as Psalm 100 commands. We must remember that just because a passage of Scripture is descriptive doesn't necessarily mean that it has nothing to say to inform my life and the practices I observe in my life.

The Importance of Worship: New Testament

The New Testament also contains many examples of worship and references to worship. When eternity breaks into time with the birth of the Incarnate Son of God the heavens were full of angels in worship. The only account of Jesus as a child centered around His being a part of the worship festivals in Jerusalem. Even as a child, Jesus described his involvement in the Temple as "being about His Father's business" (Luke 2:49). As a grown man, He made it his regular practice to go to synagogue and attend the yearly festivals of worship. Each day He rose up early to spend time in communion with the Father. Later, during his ministry, Jesus explained that worship was not geographical, but relational (John 4:21-24):

> "Woman," Jesus replied, "believe me, a time is coming when you will worship the Father neither on this mountain nor in Jerusalem. You Samaritans worship what you do not know; we worship what we do know, for salvation is from the Jews. Yet a time is coming and has now come when the true worshipers will worship the Father in the Spirit and in truth, for they are the kind of worshipers

the Father seeks. God is spirit, and his worshipers must worship in the Spirit and in truth."

Worship was an intrinsic part of the life of our Lord, not just another activity in his daily life.

The life of the early church was marked by worship, fellowship and prayer (Acts 2:42-46). The singing of worship songs by Paul and Silas had such a profound effect that the prisoners did not flee after an earthquake made escape possible and the jailer in Philippi and his entire family came to Christ (Acts 16:25). Paul declared what "reasonable worship" was in Romans 12:1-2. (We will examine this passage more carefully later in the book.) In 1 Corinthians 10:31 we are commanded to do everything for the glory of God. In Ephesians 5:19-21 and Colossians 3:16, we are commanded to sing and make melody in our hearts to the Lord always giving thanks. The giving of thanks is a key component in worship. One of the greatest worship hymns of the Incarnation is found in Philippians 2:6-11.

Another interesting passage dealing with worship is found in Hebrews 13:15: "Through Jesus, therefore, let us continually offer to God a sacrifice of praise—the fruit of lips that openly profess his name." Without going into enormous detail in the complexities of the book of Hebrews, we might say in general that the author was presenting a defense of how Jesus was the better way, the fulfillment of the old sacrificial system under Jewish law. As the author concludes his letter, he closes with a list of admonishments, similar to Paul in some of his writings. In the passage quoted, note that our worship is "through Jesus," not some self-contrived system to approach God. The only acceptable means to approach God is through His Son. Through Christ, then, we are to offer to God a "sacrifice of praise," which the author clarifies as the "fruit of lips that openly profess his name." Just as fruit is the natural result of a healthy fruit tree, so praise is the natural result of those who profess Christ as their Messiah.

When a Jewish convert of that day heard the word "sacrifice," vivid images of the sacrificial ritual would come to mind. Without trying to over simplify, here is a brief summary of four major ideas from this passage: [1] sacrifice was required from all, rich or poor. No one was exempt, [2] the offering needed to be the best they had, that is, an offering without spot or blemish, [3] the sacrificial offering was always for God's glory, never for the glory of the person offering the sacrifice, and [4] the offering was done to maintain right relationship, for the atonement of sin or for thanksgiving. If we apply these ideas to a "sacrifice of praise," we might say that praise is something that all believers are commanded to do, that our offering of praise should be the best we can offer, from a pure heart, and that it should be always done for the honor and glory of God alone. Our offering of praise is not done to atone for sin, Jesus completed that on the cross. However, as seen with the Isaiah 6 passage, we must confess our sin if we are to be able to worship God properly. Thanksgiving is intrinsically linked to worship and praise. More will be covered on this subject later.

Additional passages that speak about worship in the New Testament include words from Peter, as well as John in Revelation. Peter refers back to God's original covenant to make the people of God a kingdom of priests in 1 Peter 2:9: "But you are a chosen people, a royal priesthood, a holy nation, God's special possession, that you may declare the praises of him who called you out of darkness into his wonderful light." At least one of the implications of this passage is the power of praise as a testimony to others. And finally in Revelation of John, the culmination of time and eternity centers around the worship of the Lamb on the throne, surrounded by countless men and women from every age, every tongue and every nation, praising God and saying "Worthy is the Lamb!" Worship is central to the Scriptures from the beginning to the end. There are several wonderful books on the songs of heaven, but I would like to focus the remainder of this section on the person who is the central theme of worship in the New Testament, namely Jesus Christ.

The Centrality of Christ in Worship

As a function of language, a preposition is a word "showing the relation of a noun or a noun substitute to some other word in the sentence (the squirrel in the tree; the preposition *in* shows the relationship between the squirrel and the tree.)."[4] We use prepositions multiple times daily in speech and other forms of communication, and often overlook their importance. We can take advantage of these little words to help us gain insight into our relationship to Christ in regards to worship. This is provided not as an exhaustive listing, nor as a theological treatise, but simply to help us refocus as we think and dialogue about worship.

1. In Him

His Spirit lives in us and empowers us. The concept that we are "in Him" is a consistent way the New Testament writers describe our relationship with Christ. "For *in him* we live, and move, and exist, as even some of your own poets have said, For we are also his children" (Acts 17:28 NASB). It is "in Christ" that we have been redeemed from the old way of thinking and acting: "Therefore if anyone is *in Christ,* he is a new creature; the old things passed away; behold, new things have come" (2 Corinthians 5:17 NASB). The fact that He is in us should continually lead us away from worshiping any other. This is in one sense a great paradox: we are in Him, yet He, by the Holy Spirit, is in us! Real worship must begin with our receiving Jesus Christ as Savior and Lord; He must be in us so we can be in Him.

To Him

Worship is directed to Christ. "Now *to Him* who is able to do far more abundantly beyond all that we ask or think, according to the power that works within us, *to Him* be the glory in the church and in Christ Jesus to all generations forever and ever. Amen" (Ephesians 3:20-21 NASB). All worship, praise, honor, glory, and exaltation find their focus directed to Him. Worship directed to anything or anyone other than God is idolatry. As we worship, we must ask ourselves to whom or to what have we directed our adoration? Those leading in worship, whether through music, teaching, preaching, etc., must be especially careful because of the high visibility of the role not to redirect focus and attention on themselves.

With Him

He is present with us in worship. "For where two or three have gathered together in My name, I am there in their midst" (Matthew 18:20 NASB). He not only lives in us, but we should have an awareness of His Spirit and presence as we worship. When we received Christ we were made alive by grace: "But God, being rich in mercy, because of His great love with which He loved us, even when we were dead in our transgressions, made us alive together *with Christ* (by grace you have been saved), and raised us up *with Him*, and seated us *with Him* in the heavenly places in Christ Jesus" (Ephesians 2:4-6). We can also see that our relationship with Him must have a direct relationship with those around us: "If we say that we have fellowship *with him* while we are walking in darkness, we lie and do not do what is true; but if we walk in the light as he himself is in the light, we have fellowship with one another, and the blood of Jesus his Son cleanses us from all sin" (I John 1:6-7).

For Him

Worship is for Him. We exist for Him, as Paul stated, "yet for us there is but one God, the Father, from whom are all things and we exist *for Him*; and one Lord, Jesus Christ, by whom are all things, and we exist through Him" (1 Corinthians 8:6 NASB). Although worship has immense benefits for the worshiper, it is not for him, but for Christ. There is that sense that we are ministering to God as we worship. Our worship and ministry for Him is not because God needs it; He is self-sufficient. Our worship is that specific time in which we affirm His worthiness through obedience in recognizing that it is all for

Him. When we worship, we are joining with all creation in giving Christ the rightful place of honor.

About Him

The subject of worship is Jesus. As Peter stood to deliver
his sermon on the day of Pentecost (Acts 2:14-36), the message
from beginning to end was about Christ. Our message is to
share how God from the beginning of history has moved to
restore relationship with His creation through the death and
resurrection of His Son. Even when threatened by the Council,
Peter and John could only say, "we cannot stop speaking *about*
what we have see and heard" (Acts 4:20 NASB).

By Him

In worship we acknowledge that all things were made by Him.
"For *by Him* all things were created, both in the heavens and
on earth, visible and invisible, whether thrones or dominions
or rulers or authorities – all things have been created through
Him and for Him" (Colossians 1:16 NASB). "By Him" implies
that he is the source of all things, the originator of all creation
and "by Him" helps us to see things from God's perspective.

Through Him

We are powerless to worship without His help. "*Through Him*
then, let us continually offer up a sacrifice of praise to God, that
is the fruit of lips that give thanks to His name" (Hebrews 13:15
NASB). "All things came into being *through Him*, and apart
from Him nothing came into being that has come into being"
(John 1:3 NASB). "For *from Him and through Him and to Him* are

all things. To Him be the glory forever. Amen" (Romans 11:36 NASB). "He helps you want to obey Him and then help you do what He wants" (Phil. 2:13 TLB). There is little room for foolish pride when one realizes that it is all through Him.

Questions and Objections

I believe it is necessary to step aside briefly and address some issues and questions that have arisen through the previous discussion. I have heard people say things like, "I go worship because I have needs and I want those needs to be met." "When I go to church, I want my batteries charged." "I go to church, but I really don't get anything out of it." The desire to attend church is to be commended, but we must be careful. The goal of worship is not that my needs are met, but that we worship Christ. If we focus on "our needs," then we have redirected our attention away from the very One who is able to do anything about those needs. But, as we focus on Christ and His greatness, love, mercy, grace and forgiveness in worship, somehow He works to minister to our needs. Christ's ministry to us then, is a byproduct of worship and not the central focus.

That is not to say that needs are not important. As leaders and planners of worship services, we must speak in words that are understandable to those with whom we minister, being sensitive to their needs. But, we must not fall into the trap of thinking that we go to a particular church with a particular preacher or worship leader because that person "meets my needs." That type of thinking makes the preacher or worship leader an "idol" of sorts, and puts them in a position God never intended for them to have. God is our provider and sustainer, and we must look to Him to meet our needs. Our individual and corporate responsibility is to focus on Christ.

Another issue that needs to be addressed is "feeling like we have worshiped." We must learn to live by faith, not by feeling. Remember the most authoritative source we have at our disposal as a basis for belief is God's Word. When we say, "I didn't worship today, because I just couldn't feel anything," we are at risk of placing personal experience above God's Word. When we have a proper focus in our worship, when we respond in obedience, our feelings might eventually catch up, but to base our level and depth of worship experience on how we feel puts the cart before the horse. Remember Scripture says that the "heart is deceitful above all things and desperately wicked, who can know it?" (Jeremiah 17:9). Feelings are an important subject and will be covered more in depth later.

Let's consider another passage to underline the idea that a certain emotion indicates one has experienced true worship. Psalm 118:24 tells us "This is the day that the Lord has made, I will rejoice and be glad in it." We know it and even sing it, but we might not have thought about the fact that the psalmist' action or the psalmist's words are rooted in God's handiwork and spoken by an act of will, not feeling. He has made a choice and acts by his will. Philippians 2:13 reminds us that God will help us to want to obey Him, but we must make the choice to obey, and exercise our will. We must learn to choose to respond to God, rather than responding to God only when we "feel" something special. We must learn to choose to respond to God, rather than equate strong feelings to worship.

Questions will arise about how we are to make Christ central to our worship. Regardless what they might be, we need to remember the biblical focus of worship. Our times of worship can be laden with distractions. Perhaps a simple review of some prepositions might help us see Jesus Christ as the central focus of our corporate worship. As we gather for worship let's remember that it is to Him, and in Him; it is with Him and for Him; it is about Him, by Him and through Him! Worship centers itself, has its central focus, all on Jesus Christ. Anything less is less than worship.

Implications

Let's suppose that we are in a worship service and immediately we are reminded that He is *in us* and we are *in Him*. There is an overwhelming sense that He, himself is *with us*, and that it is *by* His love, power, and grace we can stand before Him. All that we say and do is *for Him* and *to Him*. We come to the realization that *through Him* we are offering up the sacrifice of praise for that moment. What would that look like? Our understanding of how Christ is the center of what we do is fundamental to worshiping Him in Spirit and truth. The prepositions are perhaps a type of checklist to help us refocus, rethink and recommit ourselves to what worship is all about. Why not pause right now for a worship check up?

> *Oh Father, I praise You this moment for Who You are!*
> *I thank You for Your grace, mercy, forgiveness, and for*
> *all that Jesus has done! Lord, I am in total wonder that*
> *You are in me by your Holy Spirit and that I am in*
> *Christ by what He has done! Oh God, I know it is by*

your love, power, and grace that I can even bow before You right now. In this moment, Lord, all my worship and praise is for You and to You and I know that it is only through You that I can even offer this prayer. Oh Lord, be glorified in this time of worship, prayer, and may it be a sacrifice of praise to Your Holy Name. For it is in Jesus' Name that I pray, Amen.

So, how do I worship? Do I just cross our fingers and hope for the best? No, we can be grateful that worship is not a guessing game. We worship as an act of the will, that is, we choose to respond to God's revelation of Himself.

III. Biblical Preparation for Worship

We make preparations to go on a vacation, we make a list to go to grocery store, and we get ready to go to work. Virtually everything we do requires some kind of preparation. We don't just crawl out of bed and walk into church in our pajamas. We are careful to take the time necessary so we are "ready" to walk out of the house. Just as important as these physical aspects of preparation to get ready for worship are the spiritual aspects of preparation that many times are overlooked.

In this section we will look at some passages of Scripture that can help us to "get ready" spiritually. We will look at Psalm 24 and "Going to Worship," the importance of praise and thanksgiving in Psalm 100, the need for reconciliation from Matthew 5:23-24 and Matthew 18:21-35, not taking things for granted from 2 Samuel 6:1-15, developing a vocabulary of praise from 1 Chronicles 16 and several passages covering things that impede worship.

Scripture is full of instruction about worship preparation and the following brief studies are by no means exhaustive.

Too often we read Scripture and know the content, but never get to the point where we learn to apply it in a practical way in our lives. My desire is to use these as a "jump start" for your own list and study.

Going to Worship: Psalm 24:3-4

While doing some study in Psalm 24 recently, the Lord underscored some truths and helped me understand how necessary preparation for worship really is. Let's look again at David's psalm:

1 The earth is the LORD's, and everything in it,
  the world, and all who live in it;
2 for he founded it on the seas
  and established it on the waters.

3 Who may ascend the mountain of the LORD?
  Who may stand in his holy place?
4 The one who has clean hands and a pure heart,
  who does not trust in an idol
  or swear by a false god.

5 They will receive blessing from the LORD
  and vindication from God their Savior.
6 Such is the generation of those who seek him,
  who seek your face, God of Jacob.

7 Lift up your heads, you gates;
  be lifted up, you ancient doors,
  that the King of glory may come in.
8 Who is this King of glory?
  The LORD strong and mighty,
  the LORD mighty in battle.

9   Lift up your heads, you gates;
lift them up, you ancient doors,
that the King of glory may come in.
10 Who is he, this King of glory?
The LORD Almighty—
he is the King of glory. (NIV)

Background

Psalm 24 could have been used as a song to prepare for worship, perhaps when the ark was brought to Jerusalem. It still serves as a reminder for us today about preparing for worship. Biblical scholars are uncertain as to the occasion for which the psalm was written, but celebration of God as the Great King is central to the theme. In verses 1-2 the psalmist declares that Yahweh created everything, and thus He owns it, directs its, controls it. Part of the preparation for worship is the recognition that God is the Creator and Owner of all. We really have no rights to ourselves. He is the Absolute Master of all things. He created it all and made all the rules. We are His servants to do His bidding.[5]

Once David has established that Yahweh is the great Creator-King, he has set the stage for the question, "Who may go and worship Him?" and gives the answers for that question in verses 3 - 6. Knowing that God is the All-Powerful Creator is essential in recognizing just *who* is to be worshiped. We are not approaching another important person, but God, Himself – Ruler, Creator and King. Because of who He is, not anyone and everyone may approach Him. Who may come before Him to worship? *"The one who has clean hands and a pure heart, who does not trust in an idol or swear by a false god"* (4). By clean hands, the psalmist is not talking about whether or not someone has washed their hands with soap and water, but one who has been forgiven, and one whose actions are right. Those of a pure heart come to God with pure motives. Those that come to God come trusting in Him alone as God, placing faith alone in Him. Part of the preparation for worship is right actions and pure motives. We cannot approach Holy God with unconfessed sin in our hearts and lives. We cannot approach God with alternative motives for our own selfish gain or pleasure. Realizing that He alone is Lord and Master of all helps prepare us for this.

Such trust is not without reward: "*They will receive blessing from the LORD and vindication from God their Savior*" (5). God bestows His gracious loving-kindness on them and becomes their protector. The true sons of Jacob are those who approach God without sinful actions, who come with pure motives, and consider Yahweh as their only God. The same is true for us today: coming to God rightly has its rewards: the unmerited favor of God, that is, His blessing as well as His protection, His vindication. God is responsible for my reputation; we can trust our safety and our reputations to Him for His honor and glory.

Once we realize that God is in ultimate control, once we are prepared to meet Him, then the call comes to open the gates to receive Him. This might have been an antiphonal song between the people and the leaders. They are not to "lift up their heads to an idol", but to who? The King of Glory. In this context, it is a sign of rejoicing. The repetition is for the emphasis given to the preparation. The Creator-God is the King of Glory; He is the LORD Almighty. As LORD Almighty, is the Covenant keeping God who is the most powerful and most mighty, worthy of all glory, all honor and all praise.

The psalm speaks to us today to prepare for worship. We must realize that He alone is the Creator King. We must approach Him on His terms before the gates are open and recognize Who God is: the Creator-King who is also the King of Glory, the Great Victorious Warrior. He has already conquered sin and death. He already reigns over the universe. He is Yahweh Almighty, the Covenant Keeping Creator God who desires to have a relationship with us.

Application:

What are you going to do today to prepare for worship? Will you realize that God alone is the Absolute Ruler and Owner of all things? Why not proclaim that out loud right now? Will you confess any sin and wrong motives and seek forgiveness from the Father? Preparation for worship demands that we approach God with clean hands and a pure heart, depending on Him alone as our God. *Will we make those preparations necessary that honor Who He is and What He has done?*

Praise & Thanksgiving: Psalm 100

Psalm 100

¹ Shout for joy to the LORD, all the earth. ²
Worship the LORD with gladness; come before
him with joyful songs. ³ Know that the LORD is
God. It is he who made us, and we are his; we
are his people, the sheep of his pasture. ⁴ Enter
his gates with thanksgiving and his courts with
praise; give thanks to him and praise his name. ⁵
For the LORD is good and his love endures forever; his faithfulness continues through all generations. (NIV)

With even a casual look at the first verse one can hardly
miss the power of the psalmist's command to "Shout for joy to
the Lord." The parallel statement in the following verse (worship the LORD with gladness) is given description of "how"
we are to approach with joy: "with joyful songs." The psalmist follows with the reason for such joy: knowing Yahweh (the
LORD) is God. The covenant keeping Creator who desires

to have fellowship with us is also the All-Powerful God of the Universe. Of course there is reason for rejoicing! Not only is He God, but He made us, and we are his, we are like the sheep in His pasture, those that He loves and for whom He cares. For that reason we need to "Enter his gates with thanksgiving and his courts with praise," implying that we need to spend time meditating on all that He has done and that we approach Him with a grateful heart, giving Him thanks; not complaining and gripping about this and that. It also implies that we must invest time meditating on His character and nature and come praising Him for them. Let's look at the psalm in another way:

Commands:	– Shout
	– Worship
	– Come
	– Know
	– Enter
	– give thanks
	– praise His name

How to do it:	– with joy
	– with gladness
	– with singing
	– giving thanks
	– praising His name

Why do it:	– The Lord is God
	– He is Creator
	– He is Shepherd

– The Lord is Good

– His love endures

– His faithfulness forever

When: – as we enter into His gates and courts

Who God is: – The Lord is God

– The Lord is good

How do we give thanks? For what do we give thanks? How do we praise Him? In summary:

1. **We thank God for what He has done.**
   Assignment: Share at least two things for which you are thankful to God.
2. **We praise God for who He is: His nature and character.**
   Assignment: Look through the list of names and character traits of God and pick two and in silent prayer praise God for those.

1. Loving
2. Kind
3. Merciful
4. Gracious
5. Patient
6. Forgiving
7. Faithfu
8. True
9. Just
10. Righteous
11. Unchanging

12. Creator [Is.43:15]
13. Sustainer
14. Refuge
16. Rock
17. Teacher
18. Guide
19. Corrector/ Discipliner
20. Light/Lamp [Ps. 18:28]

21. Way
22. Truth
23. Life
24. Wonderful Counselor
25. Mighty God/ Almighty
26. Healer
27. Rewarder Patient
28. Our Rest

51

29. Eternal / Everlasting
30. Substitute
31. Lawyer [Jer. 51:36/ Lam. 4:58]
32. Good / Shepherd
33. Alpha and Omega
34. Holy / Holy One [Is. 43:14]
35. Defender [Is. 43:14]
36. Bread of Heaven
37. Lord of hosts, Lord Almighty
38. Door / Gate for the Sheep
39. Branch [Zech. 3:8]
40. Priest & King [Zech 6:13]
41. Sun of Righteousness with Healing in His wings [Mal.4:2]

42. Rock / Fortress [Ps. 18:1/43:2]
43. Shield & Stronghold [Ps. 94:22]
44. Compassionate [Ps 103:8]
45. Infinite
46. Ruler
47. Impartial
48. Trustworthy
49. Everlasting
50. Tree of Life
51. Prince of Peace
52. Author of Life
53. Source of Joy
54. Savior
55. Lord of lords
56. King of kings
57. Helper
58. Judge [Lam. 4:58]
59. Redeemer
60. Friend
61. Ever Present
62. Supplier/ Provider
63. Commander
64. Son of Man/ God

65. The Upright One
66. I AM
67. Anointed One
68.Cornerstone
69. Great High Priest
70. Liberator
71. Ransom
72. Wisdom
73. Protector [Ps.121]
74. Lawgiver [Is. 33:22]

Worship and Reconciliation

Worship demands that we be reconciled one to another. Perhaps this is just a reminder to some and something that seems logical, but it is so important, it bears reviewing. Reconciliation relates to forgiving and seeking forgiveness and encompasses an enormous amount of material, but our focus will be its relation to worship.

Matthew 5, 6, and 7 comprise what is known as Jesus' Sermon on the Mount.⁶ Chapter 5, verses 3-12 are referred to as the Beatitudes, and afterwards Jesus gives commentary on how our relationship to God and others is to be lived out in the real world. Verses 13-20 deal with living out God's commandments in a way that was not being done previously. In verses 21 and following, Jesus begins several sections citing Old Testament law and tradition and then explains how the people of his day had mis-applied God's intention. It is in this context that Jesus deals with relationships and more specifically touches on reconciliation and worship in verses 23-24.

> *"Therefore, if you are offering your gift at the altar and there remember that your brother has something against you, leave your gift there in front of the altar. First go and be reconciled to your brother; then come and offer your gift* (Matthew 5:23-24 NIV).

At first, the connection may not seem very obvious, but as we begin to study, the implications begin to come to light. The "therefore" refers directly to the previous two verses:

> *You have heard that it was said to the people long ago,*
> *'Do not murder, and anyone who murders will be subject*
> *to judgment.' But I tell you that anyone who is angry*
> *with his brother will be subject to judgment. Again,*
> *anyone who says to his brother, 'Raca,' is answerable to*
> *the Sanhedrin. But anyone who says, 'You fool!' will be*
> *in danger of the fire of hell* (Matt. 5:21-22, NIV).

Jesus is stressing how important relationships are and that our attitudes toward others is just as important as our actions. In that context, Jesus goes on to say, "therefore, if you are offering your gift at the altar..." Here is where the direct tie to worship begins. The offering referred to here was not the round plate to receive offerings with which we are familiar, but "offering" in this context was that which was being offered to God, whether for the forgiveness of sin, or as a thank offering. Regardless, it was an act of worship to Jehovah. So, Jesus tells the hillside multitude that even if they are in the very act of worship and remember that they have offended someone, to stop the offering and be reconciled to that person, because worship cannot happen until reconciliation takes place. These are strong words indeed, so strong in fact, that I am concerned that we have ignored them more than obeyed them.

What does it mean to be "reconciled?" Perhaps the simplest way to understand the term is to think of reconciliation as "restored relationship." Christ provided the way that we might be "reconciled," to God, that is, that the relationship between God and man might be restored. In a similar way, when we seek to be reconciled with another person, we are seeking to restore a relationship. In our relationship with God, we confess to God that we have broken the relationship through sin and ask for His forgiveness. We were totally helpless to change the situation; we could provide no restitution or pay the debt owed to restore the relationship: Christ did it all. I once heard that confession carries the idea of "coming to agreement with," that is, when we confess our sin we agree with God in how He sees sin and that we have broken the relationship.

In order to be reconciled to the one that we have offended, there must be a recognition that we have done or said something that resulted in broken fellowship and we "confess" to that person and ask for forgiveness. It may be very possible that the other person might carry a portion of the blame, or that the offense was totally unintentional. Regardless, we must be obedient about our responsibility to take the initiative to reconcile the relationship. Even if the other party is 99% responsible in our opinion, God has commanded that we ask forgiveness for what we have done. Admitting that we have offended someone is difficult. Pride and stubbornness block our admission of guilt and sometimes restitution must be made, but the fruit of obedience to God is worth the effort.

When we ask for forgiveness, we are not to imply guilt or responsibility of the other person by saying, "I was wrong to do such and such, but you hurt me as well..," or "if this offended you..." Saying these types of statements only makes things worse. However true, these comments imply that we are more interested in sharing or avoiding blame than restoring the relationship. The need is to confess the wrong and ask forgiveness; the fewer the words the better, because many times other things will be said that might be misinterpreted and cause more damage. Many times the other person will ask for forgiveness as well, knowing that it was a mutual offense. If that occurs, grant it humbly and in no way say anything that would imply that you expected that response.

Asking for forgiveness is more than saying "I'm sorry." As I heard one pastor say, "they are sorry about it too." Sorrow is an emotion, and reflects the feeling about the situation, but forgiveness reaches down to the depths of the offense. This is why we must ask for forgiveness. If the person forgives, then express gratitude and go. If they do not, many times it is because there might be doubt that you understand the depth of the hurt or there may be doubt of the sincerity of the request. This is especially true if the offense is an often repeated one, as in the case between husbands and wives. Sometimes there may be a hesitation because there has been mutual offense and the other person is reluctant to forgive because to do so would mean asking forgiveness for their personal offenses. If the person cannot forgive, perhaps the most appropriate response would be to say something like, "I realize that this hurt you deeply and I hope and pray one day you will be able to forgive me." You must continue to respond in love to that person, regardless. You must continue to respond to that person in love, and trust that God will be at work in their heart, seeking to move them toward reconciliation with you. *Worship demands that we seek forgiveness from those we have offended.* More than ever, I am convinced the reason that worship doesn't happen in some churches is precisely because God's people are not willing to be obedient in this area. Sometime in the past someone said something or did something, and those offended are still nursing the hurt or still trying to justify some right words spoken the wrong way. The Spirit of God is a Spirit of unity and unity cannot happen with such division. The principle is that we must seek forgiveness from those we have offended, or we really cannot worship as God intended.

What about those who have offended us? An interesting and related passage is found later in Matthew 18:

> *Then Peter came to Jesus and asked, "Lord, how many times shall I forgive my brother when he sins against me? Up to seven times?" Jesus answered, "I tell you, not seven times, but seventy-seven times. "Therefore, the kingdom of heaven is like a king who wanted to settle accounts with his servants. As he began the settlement, a man who owed him ten thousand talents was brought to him. Since he was not able to pay, the master ordered that he and his wife and his children and all that he had be sold to repay the debt. "The servant fell on his knees before him. 'Be patient with me,' he begged, 'and I will pay back everything.' The servant's master took pity on him, canceled the debt and let him go. "But when that servant went out, he found one of his fellow servants who owed him a hundred denarii. He grabbed him and began to choke him. 'Pay back what you owe me!' he demanded. "His fellow servant fell to his knees and begged him, 'Be patient with me, and I will pay you back.' "But he refused. Instead, he went off and had the man thrown into prison until he could pay the debt. When the other servants saw what had happened, they were greatly distressed and went and told their master everything that had happened. "Then the master called the servant in. 'You wicked servant,' he said, 'I canceled all that debt of yours because you begged me*

57

*to. Shouldn't you have had mercy on your fellow ser-
vant just as I had on you?' In anger his master turned
him over to the jailers to be tortured, until he should
pay back all he owed. "This is how my heavenly Father
will treat each of you unless you forgive your brother
from your heart."* (Matthew 18:21-35 NIV)

While the passage in Matthew 5 deals with seeking forgiveness when we have offended someone, in Matthew 18 Jesus is
teaching about forgiving those who offend us. If we are to reflect
the nature and character of God, we must forgive. Remember
God has forgiven us, and no one will or could ever do to us what
we have done in our sin against Holy God. One of the better
explanations of forgiveness that I have encountered is found in
The Courage to Heal, by Ellen Bass and Laura Davis:

There are, then, two elements in what we call forgiveness.
One is that you give up your anger and no longer hold the
abuser to blame; you excuse them for what they did to you.
The other element is that you no longer try to get some kind
of compensation from the abuser.[7]

Forgiveness is a releasing of the consequences of what should
happen into the hands of the only One who knows all there is
to know about the situation and circumstances. He alone has
the power to do something about the offense that will be in
line with His perfect will and plan.

We forgive by an act of the will, not whether we feel like
doing so; it is an act of obedience, not a feeling. It has been said,
"I can forgive, but I can't forget." The truth is you may never
forget; but we cannot afford the cost of the continual nursing
of an offense, it will consume us. It is also something that we

continually have to do, it is a part of dying to self. Remember, Jesus' statement implied that it would be a repeated process. It might be that to be able to work through some situations you may need the assistance of a mentor or trained counselor. The important thing to remember is that as we approach the Lord in worship we should not clutch on to old hurts and unresolved offense. We must forgive those that offend us; we must release to the Lord those who offended us or we must release those offenses to the Lord.

Some might ask, "It doesn't seem fair, why should I have to go ask forgiveness and then also forgive? Isn't part of the responsibility that of the other person as well?" The answer is "yes, it is a mutual responsibility." Reconciliation is a two-sided coin, we seek forgiveness and we forgive. Why? Because it is important to God that we reflect the unity of who He is and the love He has for us. Because Jesus and the Father are one, and they desire us to be unified also.

Because we cannot adequately worship God until we ask forgiveness and forgive one another. *Worship demands that we forgive and seek forgiveness.*

What would happen in our churches if our people would begin to reconcile one with another? The great revivals of the past were marked by men and women being reconciled both with God and one another. When our desire to worship God is greater than our pride, when our desire to be fully obedient to Him is greater than our hesitancy to be reconciled to one another, I believe we will see revival in our churches. The cost of not doing so is too great.

What can we do? The first time I began to seek reconciliation from those I had offended, I literally made out a list of the individuals I needed to go to ask forgiveness. I wrote out word for word what I needed to say and called them up. We can make another list of those that have offended us and forgive and release them by an act of will to God. There exists a host of great materials on this, but the important thing is that we do it. We seek forgiveness and forgive, because worship demands that we be reconciled one with another.

Worship: Taking things for granted: 2 Samuel 6:1-15

David was a man after God's own heart, a shepherd, a warrior, and a great king, but he was also a composer, a musician and a worship leader. His attempt to bring the ark, the symbol of God's presence among His people in 2 Samuel 6:1-15 displays two basic lessons of what "not" to do if we are to worship God as He desires:

1 *David again brought together out of Israel chosen men, thirty thousand in all. 2 He and all his men set out from Baalah of Judah to bring up from there the ark of God, which is called by the Name, the name of the LORD Almighty, who is enthroned between the cherubim that are on the ark. 3 They set the ark of God on a new cart and brought it from the house of Abinadab, which was on the hill. Uzzah and Ahio, sons of Abinadab, were guiding the new cart 4 with the ark of God on it, and Ahio was walking in front of it. 5 David and the whole house of Israel were celebrating with all their might before the LORD, with songs and with harps, lyres, tambourines, sistrums and cymbals.*

6 *When they came to the threshing floor of Nacon, Uzzah reached out and took hold of the ark of God, because the*

oxen stumbled. 7 The LORD's anger burned against Uzzah because of his irreverent act; therefore God struck him down and he died there beside the ark of God.

8 *Then David was angry because the LORD's wrath had broken out against Uzzah, and to this day that place is called Perez Uzzah.*

9 *David was afraid of the LORD that day and said, "How can the ark of the LORD ever come to me?" 10 He was not willing to take the ark of the LORD to be with him in the City of David. Instead, he took it aside to the house of Obed-Edom the Gittite. 11 The ark of the LORD remained in the house of Obed-Edom the Gittite for three months, and the LORD blessed him and his entire household.*

12 *Now King David was told, "The LORD has blessed the household of Obed-Edom and everything he has, because of the ark of God." So David went down and brought up the ark of God from the house of Obed-Edom to the City of David with rejoicing. 13 When those who were carrying the ark of the LORD had taken six steps, he sacrificed a bull and a fattened calf. 14 David, wearing a linen ephod, danced before the LORD with all his might, 15 while he and the entire house of Israel brought up the ark of the LORD with shouts and the sound of trumpets.*

The moving of the ark of God to Jerusalem was to be one of the high points of King David's early accomplishments. For years the ark had been at the house of Abinadab, and perhaps the most natural question is, "How in the world did it get there and who is Abinadab?" Great questions, so let's briefly review some history found in I Samuel 4-7. As a young boy, Samuel grew up under the High Priest, Eli, after his mother and father had dedicated him to the Lord. Eli's sons were corrupt and did not follow God's commands, nor had little respect for the ark of God. When the Philistines attacked the Israelites, Hophni and Phineas, Eli's sons brought the ark of God into battle, not because they trusted in God, but more likely only as a good luck charm. They placed their trust in the ark and not the God of the ark. The battle ended with the ark being captured and Eli's sons being killed. Eli also died when he heard that the Philistines had taken the ark.

The rejoicing of the Philistines soon turned into panic as the ark was passed among their five major cities and tumors began to break out on the people. Fearing that this might be from the hand of the Israelite God, the leaders of the cities got together and decided to conduct a test. They would place the ark on a new cart with oxen that had never been yoked, place an offering of gold in the shape of the tumors they were experiencing with it and let the oxen go. If the oxen wandered about with no real direction, the tumors and trouble would be a coincidence. But if they took to the road that led to Israel, then they would know the tumors had been from the hand of God. They did what they planned and the oxen went straight down the road to Israel, to Beth Shemesh and eventually to Kiriath Jearim to the house of Abinadab on the hill. The ark remained there at least twenty years until Israel requested a king (1 Samuel 7:2), as well as the forty years that Saul was king, and until the first 7 years of David's reign in Hebron, most likely 67 years in all.

When David had unified the kingdom under his rule, he wanted to bring the ark of God to his own city, the City of David.

As we have read in the passage in 2 Samuel 6, David gathered thousands of his best soldiers, composed special psalms, and filled the air with praise and adoration to bring the ark to where he lived. David's heart was longing to be close to the symbol of the presence of Jehovah, the ark. David followed the example of the Philistines and placed the ark on a new cart, led by the sons of Abinadad, Uzzah and Ahio and began the journey to Jerusalem with great celebration and worship. Unfortunately, when the ark reached the threshing floor of Nacon, a rocky place that would have been used to beat the stalks of grain to separate it from the chaff, the oxen stumbled. Immediately Uzzah stretched out his hand to steady the ark so it would not fall off the cart and God struck him dead on the spot. Needless to say that put a damper on the celebration and they stopped the procession leaving the ark at the nearby home of Obed Edom. Three months later, David attempts the move again, but this time following the biblical mandates of using only Levites carrying the ark with poles. Again there was celebration, but this time with obedience and sacrifice.

David's failure to follow God's instructions put those around the ark in peril. All the adoration, praise, singing, and rejoicing we can possibly make cannot replace being obedient. Remember Samuel's warning to King Saul, when he failed to be obedient to what God had called him to do: "Obedience is better than sacrifice" (1 Samuel 15:22). Though David was a man "after God's own heart," even though he was the "sweet singer of Israel," even though he was doing everything with worship and praise, and even though it was done with the best intentions, it was not blessed because he failed to be obedient.

He failed to search the commandments of God and seek His direction and instruction. How many times do we ask God to bless our plans, rather than seek God's heart and direction about a specific task?

Not only is it important to seek to be obedient and follow the instructions God gives, but there is another aspect of the story that is worth pondering: Uzzah and Ahio's own attitudes. The ark had been in the possession of their household since its recovery from the Philistines (1 Samuel 6) and remained there for at least 20 years of the life of Samuel the prophet, the 40 years of Saul's reign and the first 7 years of David's kingship. There was probably never a time in their life that the ark had not been in their home. They had grown up with the ark around them all the time and most likely, it had become commonplace to them. They began to take it for granted. It lost its specialness. So much so that Uzzah felt no hesitation in reaching out to steady it. How important for those of us who virtually live in the things of God, not to begin to take them for granted, lest we be guilty of the same sin.

What does this mean for us today? All the good intentions we might have and all the emotional furor we might muster cannot replace the simple act of being obedient to what God has called us to do. Worship is not a substitute for obedience. The truth is that worship completes and expresses itself in obedience. We must never confuse the fruit of worship with worship itself. Regardless how deep our feelings of awe and wonder, or even how great our rejoicing may be, if they do not result in obedience, we have not understood what worship is and what God is doing as we worship. The goal of worship is not that "I feel better," but that we recognize more of who God is, what He has done and that the nature and character of Christ be formed in us so that God is glorified and that we respond in obedience so that the world is drawn into a relationship with Him.

Secondly, the more we invest our lives in the things of God, the greater the danger of beginning to take those things most dear to us for granted. When my wife and I were first appointed as missionaries, we were given the advice to take as many pictures of what we saw early in our months of service, because the longer that we were there, we would begin to overlook the things around us. I realized how true that was each time someone from the USA would come to visit and begin to make remarks about this thing and that and I scarcely was aware of it, since I passed by it every day.

Here is a special plea to those that lead worship: As we become busy with the details of planning and rehearsing the music, sermon preparation, microphones, projections, and pulling of countless other things that command our attention as we ready for worship, it is easy to "get the details right" but "miss the boat" because we lose that sense of "specialness" as we deal with the holy things of God. None are exempt from the temptation of taking the things of God for granted, but for those who are called to a specific public ministry, the danger is especially great. Even if you are "just an ordinary member" of a church, it is possible become so accustomed to what is happening in worship that one can forget the privilege of being in corporate worship, or even indifferent to the moving of God's Spirit.

Developing a vocabulary of Praise: 1 Chronicles 16

Let's look at another interesting passage about worship in the life of David, a man after God's own heart. Our focus here is simply the various commands and verbs the kings uses as he celebrates the moving of the Ark of the Covenant. As you read, notice the various and specific commands he uses which have been put in bold italic print.

1 Chronicles 16 (ASV)

¹And they brought in the ark of God, and set it in the midst of the tent that David had pitched for it: and they offered burnt-offerings and peace-offerings before God. ²And when David had made an end of offering the burnt-offering and the peace-offerings, he blessed the people in the name of Jehovah. ³And he dealt to every one of Israel, both man and woman, to every one a loaf of bread, and a portion of flesh, and a cake of raisins.

⁴And he appointed certain of the Levites to minister before the ark of Jehovah, and to celebrate and to thank and praise Jehovah, the God of Israel: ⁵Asaph the chief, and second to him Zechariah, Jeiel, and Shemiramoth, and Jehiel, and Mattithiah, and Eliab, and Benaiah, and Obed-edom, and Jeiel, with psalteries and with harps; and Asaph with cymbals, sounding aloud; ⁶and Benaiah and Jahaziel the priests with trumpets continually, before the ark of the covenant of God. ⁷Then on that day did David first ordain to give thanks unto Jehovah, by the hand of Asaph and his brethren.

⁸ O *give thanks* unto Jehovah, *call* upon his name;
Make known his doings among the peoples.
⁹ *Sing unto him*, sing praises unto him;
Talk ye of all his marvellous works.
¹⁰ *Glory ye* in his holy name;
Let the heart of them *rejoice* that seek Jehovah.
¹¹ *Seek ye Jehovah* and his strength;
Seek his face evermore.
¹² *Remember his marvelous works* that he hath done,
His wonders, and the judgments of his mouth,
¹³ O ye seed of Israel his servant,
Ye children of Jacob, his chosen ones.
¹⁴ He is Jehovah our God;
His judgments are in all the earth.
¹⁵ *Remember his covenant* for ever,
The word which he commanded to a thousand generations,
¹⁶ The covenant which he made with Abraham,
And his oath unto Isaac,
¹⁷ And confirmed the same unto Jacob for a statute,
To Israel for an everlasting covenant,
¹⁸ Saying, Unto thee will I give the land of Canaan,
The lot of your inheritance;
¹⁹ When ye were but a few men in number,
Yea, very few, and sojourners in it;
²⁰ And they went about from nation to nation,
And from one kingdom to another people.
²¹ He suffered no man to do them wrong;
Yea, he reproved kings for their sakes,
²² Saying, Touch not mine anointed ones,
And do my prophets no harm.
²³ *Sing unto Jehovah*, all the earth;
Show forth his salvation from day to day.

²⁴ ***Declare his glory*** among the nations,
His marvelous works among all the peoples.
²⁵ For great is Jehovah, and greatly to be praised:
He also is to be feared above all gods.
²⁶ For all the gods of the peoples are idols:
But Jehovah made the heavens.
²⁷ Honor and majesty are before him:
Strength and gladness are in his place.
²⁸ ***Ascribe unto Jehovah***, ye kindreds of the peoples,
Ascribe unto Jehovah glory and strength;
²⁹ ***Ascribe unto Jehovah the glory*** due unto his name:
Bring an offering, and ***come before him***:
Worship Jehovah in holy array.
³⁰ ***Tremble before him***, all the earth:
The world also is established that it cannot be moved.
³¹ ***Let the heavens be glad***, and ***let the earth rejoice***;
And ***let them say among the nations, Jehovah reigneth***.
³² ***Let the sea roar***, and the fulness thereof;
Let the field exult, and all that is therein;
³³ Then shall the trees of the wood sing for joy before Jehovah;
For he cometh to judge the earth.
³⁴ ***O give thanks unto Jehovah***; for he is good;
For his loving kindness endureth for ever.
³⁵ And say ye, ***Save us, O God of our salvation***,
And gather us together and deliver us from the nations,
To give thanks unto thy holy name,
And to ***triumph in thy praise***.
³⁶ ***Blessed be Jehovah***, the God of Israel,
From everlasting even to everlasting.
And all the people said, Amen, and praised Jehovah.
³⁷So he left there, before the ark of the covenant of Jehovah, Asaph and his brethren, to minister before the

ark continually, as every day's work required; [38]and Obed-edom with their brethren, threescore and eight; Obed-edom also the son of Jeduthun and Hosah to be doorkeepers; [39]and Zadok the priest, and his brethren the priests, before the tabernacle of Jehovah in the high place that was at Gibeon, [40]to offer burnt-offerings unto Jehovah upon the altar of burnt-offering continually morning and evening, even according to all that is written in the law of Jehovah, which he commanded unto Israel; [41]and with them Heman and Jeduthun, and the rest that were chosen, who were mentioned by name, to give thanks to Jehovah, because his loving kindness endureth for ever;[42]and with them Heman and Jeduthun with trumpets and cymbals for those that should sound aloud, and with instruments for the songs of God; and the sons of Jeduthun to be at the gate. [43]And all the people departed every man to his house: and David returned to bless his house.

Application

Even a casual study reveals that in the sections above David is quoting from Psalm 105:1-15 and Psalm 96:1-13 and a few other Psalms. They were songs of praise, but at the same time, songs that reminded the Israelites of God's promise to Abraham, His protection and provision and His special purpose for them as a people. Rather than study the Psalms themselves in their context, what is important here is how David used them in the context of a worship service.

Since he was not in the priestly tribe or family of Levites, he was not allowed to function in the daily rites of sacrificial worship. But as King, relocating the Ark of God, there arose a rare occasion to participate in worship leading. In that function, the special combination of psalms serve to instruct by recalling the great events of Israel's past and reminding them of the greatness of the God that brought it all about. Not only did these psalms serve to remind them, but they also served a prophetic role to command them to respond to what God had done in their lives. This response was worship.

Look at the myriad of commands David links with praising God for who He is and thanking God for what He has done: give thanks, call, make known, sing, talk, glory, rejoice, seek, remember, sing, show forth, declare, ascribe, bring, come, worship, and tremble. These commands cover public and private expressions of praise and gratitude, testimony and worship. It is our responsibility to make these a reality as we gather as the Body of Christ to worship Him. Although they were given to a group, the only way they can be carried out is if the individuals in that group take up their part in carrying them out. Congregational response is the unifying of individual response in obedience to what God commands.

Our congregations must learn to accept the personal responsibility each individual has before God as each one enters to worship. Accepting personal responsibility comes from study and from teaching, year after year, generation after generation. We cannot assume that because we have learned to worship that our loves ones will automatically follow in full understanding. Over and over again, the command from God to the children of Israel in the desert was "teach your children..." Teach them to give thanks, to sing, to glory in the Lord, to seek His face, to rejoice in the Lord, to remember all that He has done, to declare His greatness, ascribe Him glory, to come before Him, to worship and tremble in awe at His great majesty.

As we look at all of these, we must ask ourselves, *"How many of these are true in my life? Do I give thanks? Am I making known His deeds? Do I sing to Him in worship for His glory? Do I talk of His greatness and salvation? Do I rejoice in who He is? Do I ascribe the glory due His Name?"* We need to learn the vocabulary of worship, not to show off our knowledge of Scripture or to impress others, but to begin to learn how great and how awesome is the God we serve!

Things that Impede Worship

What are those things that impede worship or make worship more distant? Of course if
we were to answer that, the first response would be "sin," and that would be absolutely correct. Sin separates us from fellowship with God and obviously from worshiping God. But are there certain attitudes that we may not immediately recognize as "sin" that plant seeds of separation with our communion with God? Again, a list could be made rather quickly: anger, impatience, worry, ungratefulness, and the list could go on. Certainly this is not exhaustive, but I would like to focus on these three: ungratefulness, wrong focus, and pride.

Ingratitude
Gratitude is a key component of biblical worship. Please consider the following passages:

Psalm 100: 1-5
> *Shout for joy to the LORD, all the earth. Worship the LORD with gladness; come before him with joyful songs. Know that the LORD is God. It is he who made us, and we are his we are his people, the sheep of his pasture. Enter his gates with thanksgiving and his courts with praise;* **give thanks** *to him and praise his name. For the LORD is good and his love endures forever; his faithfulness continues through all generations.*

In Psalm 100, the psalmist commands our worship to be a joyful proclamation of recognition of the fact that God is in control, that we praise Him for who He is and thank Him for what He has done.

1 Chronicles 16:4
> *He appointed some of the Levites to minister before the ark of the LORD, to make petition, to* **give thanks,** *and to praise the LORD, the God of Israel:*

In this passage David assigns some of the Levites to continually give thanks before the Lord.

2 Chronicles 20:21
> *After consulting the people, Jehoshaphat appointed men to sing to the LORD and to praise him for the splendor of his holiness as they went out at the head of the army,*

*saying: **"Give thanks** to the LORD, for his love endures forever."*

— Jehoshaphat sends out the Levites in chorus to sing, giving thanks for what God is going to do, even before the battle begins.

Nehemiah 12:31

***I had the leaders of Judah go up on top of the wall. I also assigned two large choirs to give thanks.** One was to proceed on top of the wall to the right, toward the Dung Gate.*

— Nehemiah sends two choirs on top of the newly rebuilt walls to give thanks as part of the dedication of the newly finished wall.

1 Corinthians 10:16

*Is not the cup of thanksgiving for which we **give thanks** a participation in the blood of Christ? And is not the bread that we break a participation in the body of Christ?*

— Paul shows that part of the purpose of the Lord's Supper was to remember and give thanks for what Christ did on the cross.

1 Thessalonians 5:18

***give thanks** in all circumstances, for this is God's will for you in Christ Jesus.*

— Paul commands that we be thankful in (not necessarily for) everything, explaining that it is God's will.

Revelation 11:17

*saying: **"We give thanks** to you, Lord God Almighty, the One who is and who was, because you have taken your great power and have begun to reign.*

— Finally, when we get to heaven, will we have finally said enough of our thanks? No, in fact, not until then will we begin to grasp what Christ did for us.

So if gratitude is such an integral part of worship, then those things which hinder gratitude are those things which impede our worship. Question: What is the opposite of gratitude? Answer: *Ingratitude,* or the neglecting to recognize and relate thanks to God for what He does and is doing. While my wife, Kathy and I were talking about this, she shared an insight that I believe is a key to gratitude: learning contentment. Ingratitude can express itself in a "lack of contentment." This can manifest itself in many ways, but perhaps the most common is a lack of contentment with God's provision. Paul said in I Timothy 6:6 *"but godliness with contentment is great gain."* Why would this be so? Contentment is one way to express gratitude for the provision of God.

If you were to give a birthday gift to a friend and they replied: "Oh, thank you for the gift, but what I really wanted was the other model," how would you feel? Would you feel that the "thank you" given was sincere? Of course not. Gratitude, by its very nature, manifests appreciation for what has been given. When we complain about what we don't have to others, but are telling God "thank you for your provision," we are not manifesting true appreciation for God's provision. Paul put it this way: "Do everything without complaining or arguing, so that you may become blameless and pure, children of God without fault in a crooked and depraved generation, in which you shine like stars in the universe" (Philippians 2:14-15).

Ingratitude can also express itself by simple neglect. Neglect allows the priority of one thing to push another aside so that it remains undone. It can also be an expression of complete forgetfulness. I have made promises to my wife that I would do a specific thing, but allowed other things "more urgent" get "in the way" and sometimes even make me forget completely that I had previously told her I would do them. Neglect can be more than a lack of love, it can also be an expression of ingratitude.

The cure is first confess our ingratitude and claim His forgiveness and grace. Then we purposefully and thoughtfully review the greatness of God and His creation, His work, the history of how He worked through the children of Israel, and the history of how He has worked in our lives. We are fairly good to praise God for supplying a great need, whether restored health, financial help, or some other miraculous working of God, — and we should be! But sometimes we forget that the greatest miracle of all is salvation itself! We may need to take some time to write out what God has done and keep a "thanksgiving notebook" that we review and update on a regular basis. I'm more than confident that creative people can think of ways to include children on such projects so that they are actively involved in regularly expressing thanks. What a heritage we can leave our children — a record of the faithfulness of God! If we fail to develop a consistent way of sharing gratitude to God, we run the risk of developing an attitude of ingratitude and ingratitude hinders our worship.

As we continue down the path of ingratitude, the next thing we will encounter will be a spirit of *entitlement*, exhibiting the concept that God owes us a blessing, or a good church, fewer complaining church members, good heath, or a host of other things we desire. We begin to think of all the "sacrifices" we have made to follow Christ, or that since we are being obedient, God should reward our good behavior. One of the misconceptions about entitlement is that it fails to take into account that suffering is a normal part of following Christ. Paul put it this way in Philippians 3:10, "that I may know Him and the power of His resurrection and the fellowship of sharing in His sufferings." We are more prepared to follow a Christ that enjoys the comforts of life more than a Christ who has a commitment to the cross. If anyone were "entitled" to the world's best, would not it have been the very Creator of it all? Paul in Philippians shares that "though he was God, he did not consider equality with God something to be grasped, but made himself nothing, taking on the very nature of a servant, being made in human likeness and be found in appearance as a man, he humbled himself by being obedient to death, even death on a cross" (2:6-8). The cure for entitlement is to "let this attitude be in you which was in Christ Jesus" (Philippians 2:5). Our realization that we owe everything, even life and breath, and even more the very salvation of our souls and an eternity in heaven with God, should remind us that it was not because we were so special, but because His love was so great. We deserved death and separation from God.

When God doesn't respond in the way we think He should, we sink to the next level of *doubt and resistance* to God's plan.[8] As long as things are going well, it is relatively easily to follow Christ. But when we've expected God to do something and He "fails" to come through according to the way we thought He should, then we begin to think that He might not have our best interests in mind after all. If He really did love us that much, why would He let us go through such things? Doubt and resistance begin to creep in. We even begin to think, "How can I really trust God? If He would allow this, what would happen if I were to completely surrender to Him?" Selective obedience is often seen at every level, but especially now. God might not be the "friend" that we thought He was.

If we continue down this path, the result will lead to *indifference*. At this point, one could care less what God does or what one does; worship is not a relevant topic. One may attend church occasionally, but probably won't continue to attend consistently. There is no expectation of what God may do, because God is no longer even on the radar. For those who are trapped by indifference, worship is a cold exercise for those who have not learned the cruel truth that worship is useless. When Jesus performed miracles in Korazin and Bethsaida the people seemed to be indifferent. Perhaps it was something like this that prompted Jesus to say in Luke 10:13, "Woe to you, Korazin! Woe to you, Bethsaida! For if the miracles that were performed in you had been performed in Tyre and Sidon, they would have repented long ago, sitting in sackcloth and ashes." How tragically sad that the Creator of the universe can pass by and someone could be totally indifferent. Only the Holy Spirit can draw someone out of that pit, but praise God, He can do it.

So we see that ingratitude is a path that will destroy our worship and can render our lives unfruitful. Let's commit ourselves to gratitude, from the small things to the large, overflowing in thankfulness to God for who He is and what He has done and will continue to do!

I listen to several podcasts each week, one of which is Ravi Zacarias, the Christian apologist whom I have grown to greatly admire. One particular week his message was on "Worship" and my ears picked up. I wondered if he would elaborate on the Isaiah 6 passage, or John 4; I was ready to hear what this godly man with so much insight would say. I can say that I was disappointed at first that he began to read out of the book of Malachi. Malachi? I thought, "oh well, let's hear what he has to say." Malachi 1:2 begins like this: "I have loved you," says the Lord. But you say, "How have You loved us?" Then it really began to dawn on me: they had

gotten so complacent about their relationship with God, that they had even forgotten all that He had done for them. Active gratitude can help prevent this from happening in our lives, and as we teach this to our children, we may be able to help avoid it in their lives as well.

Five Simple Steps I Can Take to Overcome Ingratitude

First, begin a list of things for which you are thankful; be as comprehensive as possible. Start it with some phrase or Scripture, such as: "Father, I want to thank You for_____". Go over it daily in your daily devotions and try to add to it weekly. Surely God has done something during the week for which you are grateful, in addition to what you have written down on your list. Second, every time you catch yourself complaining, or expressing lack of contentment, go over your list. Take a few moments to mediate on each item. Every time you are caught in a group that is complaining, if you cannot easily remove yourself from the situation, try to go over your list mentally. Third, before you go to worship on Sunday, go over your list again. Four, when appropriate, verbalize your gratitude to God to others. (Not like the Pharisee, "God, I thank you that I'm so good...," but simple sincere gratitude.) Lastly, share gratitude to at least one person everyday. Although this is not directly related to showing gratitude to God, it continues to help us focus on being grateful and can actually encourage others to do the same.

Confusing Worship with Something Else, or Missing the Point of Worship

C. S. Lewis spoke about how dogs generally won't look to what you point at with your finger, instead, they go sniff the finger, missing your intentions. Worship, for many, is like that. They begin to focus on worship itself, rather than the God to whom all worship belongs. As I teach and converse with students about worship, one of the most common things I find is the fascination with the "feelings" of worship. There is a sense that if they didn't feel the same emotional high they felt in a past experience they judged to be "great worship" then they have not experienced real worship. Worship, like love, is reflected more in commitment than feeling. Like the dog, they keep sniffing the finger, rather than see the real focus.

If we were to get specific about what some of these "fingers" are, I would start with the following:

The feeling and emotions of worship. Not that experiencing a specific feeling is wrong, but our emotional state is not the measure of our worship. Our loving obedience to what God has called us to do is the true measure of our worship

Worshiping "worship" itself. Just as some people become so infatuated with love that they "fall in love" with love, more than a real person, so some begin to worship "worship," or at least those things related to it.

Worshiping a musical style or the music itself. A single musical style can no more capture all of who God is and how He communicates with His children anymore than one single language and culture can. Worship is not restricted to any single music style.

The structures of worship. Whether the format of a worship service might be more liturgical or the free church tradition, structures are like the frame of a picture and only facilitate the display; they were never intended to outshine the painting.

The individual parts of worship. Unfortunately, many people today use the word "worship" as a synonym for the word "music." Worship is not just the music; worship must include the praying, the reading of God's Word, the offering, the testimonies, and yes the exposition of Scripture in addition to the musical participation or our understanding of worship is not fully biblical.

Focusing on the personalities leading worship. Worship leaders should best be called "lead worshipers." Pastors, and virtually anyone that is in a publically visible position in worship, can become the focus of attention. Admiration and respect can develop into something totally askew from God's purposes, especially in situations in which individuals that come to worship come with deep emotional needs and hurts and those in leadership positions seem to "have all the answers."

What might be some solutions for these problems? The leadership sincerely desires that everyone from old to young worship God with their heart, mind, soul, and spirit, and yet many still focus on the wrong thing. Without trying to simplify the issues too much, here is a starting list:

We must teach what biblical worship is and not assume that everyone understands. I cannot remember when there has ever been such an emphasis on worship in my lifetime. We cannot afford the luxury of assuming the members of our churches have a true biblical understanding of worship; we must start from square one.

Those that lead worship must be living models of biblical worship. The temptation to follow the "worship leading style" of someone is tremendous for many young leaders. They imitate the words and actions, but many times have not paid the price of deepening their personal relationship with Christ so that their worship is an outgrowth of that relationship. They have not paid the price to hone their musical or communication skills to lead effectively and without distraction.

We must learn the principle of the unity of the body. I like what Dr. John Hopkins, Dean of the School of Fine Arts at Samford University said, that "we need not so much a table for every person, but a place for every person at the table." The model of worship in heaven is one where every tribe, tongue, and nation are gathered around the throne of God in worship. Individuality melds together by the grace of God in worship. Multi-generational worship is a healthy model for children

81

to see how their parents and grandparents respond in praise and adoration to the God who created the universe and who redeems for eternity. This happens when we are more committed to making God the focus of our worship than making the dictates of personal style and taste the focus.

We must develop a deep hunger and thirst to know God better and respond in loving obedience through personal study of God's Word and prayer. However simple, this principle cannot be underestimated. We cannot share what we do not have and we cannot lead where we have not been. It is my prayer that we begin the process of focusing on what worship is, and teach it to others by personal application.

Pride: The Unseen Enemy

Hezekiah led one of the greatest returns to the worship of Jehovah in all of history of the divided kingdoms. His father, Ahaz, had completely abandoned the worship of Jehovah and led the nation into complete ruin and disaster over a period of 16 long years. Hezekiah's grandfather, Jotham, though not perfect, had been more determined to follow the Lord: *"Jotham grew powerful because he was determined to please the Lord his God"* (2 Chron. 27:6 NET). The influence and heritage of the grandfather as well as great grandfather (Uzziah) perhaps made the difference in young Hezekiah's life. As a young adult of 25, his first act as king was to reopen the Temple, have the priests and Levites consecrate themselves and clean out the Temple.

After the temple had been re-consecrated, the young king assembled the city officials for worship and to consecrate themselves to the Lord.

> *"As they began to offer the sacrifice, they also began to sing to the Lord, accompanied by the trumpets and the musical instruments of King David of Israel. The entire assembly worshiped, as the singers sang and the trumpeters played. They continued until the burnt sacrifice was completed"* (2 Chron. 29:27-28 NET).

Notice that the singing was part of the sacrifice and that they all worshiped. This was not for entertainment or show; this was a re-consecration to the Lord so that the leadership of the city would realize God was their ultimate authority. This preceded their own personal sacrifices for worship (v. 31) initiating the regular sacrifices in the Temple once again.

Hezekiah's next act as king was to send out messengers throughout the lands of all 12 tribes inviting them to return to the Lord and celebrate the Passover in Jerusalem. (Some did return, but most did not. Little did they realize that in less than five years the Assyrians would carry the Northern Kingdom into captivity.) The celebration of Passover initiated by leadership was almost always tied to great revival in the Old Testament and this was no different. Not only was the celebration great, they decided to extend the length another entire week. Afterward, they destroyed the other altars dedicated for pagan worship. The king called for the restoration of the offerings so that the priests and Levites could do the work of the Lord without having to work outside of their assigned responsibilities and God richly blessed.

Rumors began to fly that the Assyrians were about to invade the land, so Hezekiah began to make preparations: re-routing water supplies, manufacturing weapons and rebuilding the walls. The representative of the Assyrian king came mocking Jehovah God and declaring that the situation was hopeless, that no god could stop the powerful Assyrian king. Hezekiah cried out to God in prayer and God struck down the Assyrian army, leaving the few survivors to return to Assyria in shame. Revival had come, the people and their king were worshiping and depending on God. It seemed as if no enemy could touch them.

However there was one enemy that Hezekiah failed to see. It was the same enemy that had defeated his great grandfather, Uzziah, years before— pride. Listen to what Scripture says about Uzziah:

> *"But once he (Uzziah) became powerful, his pride destroyed him. He disobeyed the Lord his God"* (2 Chron. 26:16).

Now compare that to Hezekiah:

> *"In those days Hezekiah was stricken with a terminal illness. He prayed to the Lord, who answered him and gave him a sign confirming that he would be healed. But Hezekiah was ungrateful; he had a proud attitude, provoking God to be angry at him..."* (2 Chron. 32:24-25).

How do we know that Hezekiah was proud? Later when visitors from Babylonia came to see him, he tried to impress them with everything he had and had done. Verse 31 of the same chapter offers great commentary about the visit and Hezekiah's response: *"God left him alone to test him, in order to know his true motives."* Not long after, Isaiah the prophet declared that everything the visitors had seen would be carried off to Babylonia. No where in the biblical account did Hezekiah explain that he had recovered from his illness as a direct result of God's gracious intervention. He might have thought that because he had done so much, God owed him his health. The spirit of entitlement very well could have been the source of leading the king toward his fall.

Pride had been the enemy of worship in the life of Uzziah, as he disregarded God's commands to worship. God struck him with leprosy and he could never enter the temple to worship again (2 Chron. 26:16-23). Sadly, all the reforms Hezekiah led, the revival he promoted, and the great victory over the Assyrians could not prepare him for the enemy he did not see, his own pride and the consequences of letting that pride rule his actions. Hezekiah's greatest battle was not lost during difficulty, but in prosperity, looking to what he saw as his own accomplishments, rather than seeing God's grace and blessing.

So what? That's a tragic story, but what difference does mean for me, thousands of years later? I'm glad you asked. I imagine that books could be written, or may even have been written on these chapters in 2 Chronicles. To get the entire background, go back and study the parallel passages in 2 Kings

15-20. I would like to highlight some lessons as they might apply to worship and leading worship.

First, God decides what worship is and how to do it; we don't. Uzziah learned the hard way and we can learn from his mistake. Next, worshiping anyway we please has serious consequences. Again, Uzziah serves as an example of what not to do. Third, past victories do not guarantee future ones. We must praise and thank God for what He has done in the past, but there is never a time when we can let down our guard, thinking that we cannot be defeated. Hezekiah had displayed amazing spiritual leadership in worship and in war, yet was totally caught off guard by his own pride. Fourth, times of blessing can be the times we are most vulnerable. We cry out to God in our need, and we should. Yet, when we do not sense great need, it is easy to forget that we still are dependent on the Father for our "daily bread." Fifth, pride is an enemy of everything God wants to do in our life. It is directly opposed to the will and purposes of God. One of the fruits of pride is a spirit of entitlement, thinking because we have done so much, God owes us. Lastly, sincere praise and thanksgiving can help remind us who God is and help us remember what He has done. This allows us to avoid the problem of pride and a spirit of entitlement taking control of our actions and attitudes.

IV. Biblical Understandings in Leading Corporate Worship

For a number of years it has been my privilege to study and teach on worship and worship related matters. Out of the questions and discussions with students and others some questions seemed to be repeated more than others. The following material came from these discussions and I trust will be helpful. In addition to discussions on congregational song and leading worship, there is a discussion on the difference between worship and entertainment, ministering to the Lord, a character study of leadership failure, and a brief history of congregational worship.

What Is Congregational Worship?

I realize the question of what congregational worship is may seem obvious or perhaps even not worth considering, but Mark Galli, Senior Editor for *ChristianityToday,* addresses this issue in part in his article, "The End of Christianity as We Know It." Listen to what Galli has to say:

> If religious experience is something that a drug can induce even more easily than spiritual ritual and disciplines, it may be time, for example, to rethink what many churches are trying to do on Sunday morning: create a memorable "worship experience.""[9]

I would encourage the reader to search out his entire article, but I believe it is time to revisit the subject. I would like to just briefly touch on some aspects that might help us reconsider what it means when we gather together for "church."

What is congregational worship? I will throw out my two cents and perhaps it will at least get the conversation started.

> *Congregational worship is more than just a group of individuals having quiet times in the same place. It is the Body of Christ gathered together in unity and diversity centering adoration on the King of kings and Lord of lords and responding in obedience to Him. The emphasis is not on "my personal experience," but "our obedient response" to His revealed nature and character.*

To understand where all of this started, I must go back to an email from Rev. Eric Benoy, our librarian at the Seminary, who really helped me begin to start thinking about "congregational worship."

> We gather together for corporate worship; a group of people to do something in one accord. If that is the case, then why do some worship leaders today want to make corporate worship a personal experience? It is oxymoronic in a way. If we have gathered intentionally for corporate worship, then should we not then be striving for a corporate offering of praise, adoration, et al and hear from God as a body of believers? We have come together specifically to be the church gathered; to worship and become equipped to be the church scattered.[10]

Besides being our librarian, and a fine one at that, Eric is a pastor and a dear godly friend whose opinion is worth the time to ponder. I'm not sure I had spent much time thinking about the efforts being made to make "corporate worship" a "personal experience," but the more I began to mull over the idea in my mind, the more I began to see some of the possible ramifications of the idea.[11]

Biblical worship is God-centered. Scripture describes it as "in Him, through Him, by Him, to Him, and about Him," that is, the focus of worship is Christ, not our tastes, style, opinions, etc. If we look at the Isaiah 6 model, as God takes the initiative and reveals Himself, the prophet not only sees the revealed nature of God, but sees himself as God sees him, sinful and unclean. He confesses and is forgiven and the prophet is able to hear God's voice: "Whom shall I send? Who will go for us?" Worship is then completed by obedient response as Isaiah responds, "Here am I, Lord, send me!"

How does all that fit into a congregational setting? A great question. The idea of the "congregation" is in reference to the "church," not the church building, but the Body of Christ, the Bride of Christ. This body, whose Head is Christ, Himself, is seen in worship in the book of Revelation as thousands upon thousands are gathered around the Lamb on His throne. He is the one central and only focus. Angelic beings circle around Him declaring His nature and glory, hallowed saints cast their crowns toward the One who is worthy. If we could look around at the worshipers in heaven, we would notice that it is multigenerational worship: not only are there throngs of believers from all the ages, generation after generation, but old and young. It is also multi-cultural worship: tribes from every tongue and nation lifting praise and adoration to God (Revelation 15 and 19).

In Acts 2:42 we read that "They were devoting themselves to the apostles' teaching and to fellowship, to the breaking of bread and to prayer" (NET). There may be discussion as to what exactly is meant by each of these four activities, but central to each is the fact that they were done corporately. Paul deals with the abuses of the agape feast and the Lord's Supper in I Corinthians 11, emphasizing the need for self-examination, so that when they came together they would not be condemned. It is not by accident that he then deals with Spiritual gifts and explains that they are each members of Christ's body, each with different gifts for the building of the body. In I Corinthians 14, Paul deals with the fact that worship was participatory: "When you come together, each one has a song, has a lesson, has a revelation, has a tongue, has an interpretation. Let all these things be done for the strengthening of the church" (14:26 NET).

The focus was not on building up the individual participating, but the body as a whole.

It may be that because we live in a culture that prizes individualism we look at Scripture with "individualistic" lenses. While it is true that we come to Christ as individuals, our "cultural lenses" may filter the importance of seeing ourselves as the Body with Christ as its Head and as the Bride preparing herself for the Bridegroom. Though we are aware this theme is central to the New Testament idea of the church, what implications are there to worship? Where does the church "see" itself as the "Body of Christ" and not just a group of individuals? Is it not as believers gather for worship and join together unifying their focus on the Risen Lord?

Seeing ourselves as the Body of Christ is not to demean personal experience, but a help to guard against allowing our focus to shift to "our" personal experience rather than on who Christ is and what He as done. If we are not careful the desire to achieve a "personal" worship experience becomes a goal in and of itself and misses the object for which the worship should have been directed. We can begin to desire the "experience" more than the "Savior." Brian Wren put it this way in his book, *Praying Twice: The Music and Words of Congregational Song:*

Oh, I'm thinking of me praising Jesus, and loving the feeling I feel.

When I think of his touch I am feeling so much

that tomorrow I'll praise him for real.[12]

Corporate worship can help us avoid the "me and mine" mentality and can help us see ourselves as Christ sees us. Being mindful that we are part of the Body can also help us avoid delusions of our own importance before God. This is especially needful for those who are in positions of leadership in worship; it is too easy to fall into the trap of self-aggrandizement. When our focus is on worshiping as the Body of Christ, we are less likely to define our worship experience by the limited standards of our own experience. Personal preference is surrendered for the good of the whole.

What is the role of personal experience? The responsibility of every believer is to maintain a right relationship with the Father, to confess known sin, receive forgiveness and continue to grow and deepen the relationship. As we come together in worship, we come prepared to meet with Him who loved us enough to die to restore the relationship that He knew we so desperately needed. We come together as members of the Body of Christ, different in gifts and abilities, but all functioning for the good of the Body. As we worship, we reflect the "unity in diversity" that is His body.

In corporate worship can we see the unity of focusing everything on Christ. In the same way that a wheel is recognizable as a wheel when each of its spokes is rightly related to the hub, so the members of the Body are recognizable when rightly related to Christ. Just as a wheel is more than a collection of spokes hub and rims, corporate worship is more than a group of believers in the same room at the same time.

So now what? What difference does this mean in relation to what should happen on Sunday morning as we gather together? Glad you asked. For a start, let's consider the following:

1. We must teach what biblical worship is and isn't. There are still many people that believe that "the music is the worship…"

2. Personal worship is indispensable. We must feed daily on God's Word; we must immerse ourselves in His presence in prayer. There are no substitutes for personal time with the Father.

3. Personal worship is not a substitute for corporate worship. We are baptized into the Body of Christ and are members of His body. There is no biblical idea of a member of the body existing apart from the body.

4. Corporate worship must facilitate worship that centers itself around Jesus Christ as His Body. The focus of corporate worship is not a focus on personal experience.

5. We must begin to learn what it means to live and worship as the Body of Christ.

6. Personal preference is willingly subjugated for the good of the whole body.

What Makes a Song "Congregational?"

In any given worship service, some songs "sing" for lack of a better term, while others never seem to get off the ground. Why? There are a host of answers, but one overlooked solution is analyzing the song to see if it is congregational. What makes a song "congregational?" The following considerations are provided to help answer the question:

1. Is the text biblical? The text must be consistent with biblical truth. Today there has been a re-awakening of paraphrased biblical texts and older traditional texts set to fresh melodies and "troped" songs like "O the Wonderful Cross", which adds amplifies Mason's "When I Survey" and "My Chains Are Gone" which modifies "Amazing Grace." (Tropes were melodic and textual additions to well-know chant melodies that took on a life of their own during the Middle Ages.) With these types of additions to older established song texts, a need may occasionally rise for evaluation theologically of the new text being added, that is, a "theological filter." Denominational hymnals are required to go through a committee prepared to filter theological weaknesses and errors. Not only do "troped" songs need to be evaluated theologically, but many of the recently composed songs used in worship have not been analyzed for theological content, even though they are based on biblical themes.

The music industry itself is partly to blame for this since it seems more market driven, as are the radio stations which depend on maintaining their nich market of listeners and feeding their wants through the airwaves. Most of the time their emphasis is the "latest and greatest," since that's how they stay in business, not by being a theological filter;.

With the advancement in home recording systems and the internet, the need for theological filters is even more necessary, since virtually anyone with access to the equipment can put a song on *YouTube* without any doctrinal accountability. Many of the artists are sincere believers, but have no formal theological training. There are some contemporary artists that are more careful than others. The emphasis is that before a song in used in a congregational setting, it needs to be checked to see if the theology expressed is consistent with what Scripture teaches. (Remember what has been stated earlier: just because the Bible mentions something, doesn't necessarily mean it teaches it.)

2. Does the text speak to experiences common to believers? The joy of conversion, the greatness and majesty of God are common experiences to those who name Christ as Lord and Savior because they are ones in which the congregation may identify. Songs that tell of a personal experience that are unique to a particular person, or just a small group may serve well as songs of testimony, but may not be the most appropriate for the congregation. We must remember that worship is not entertainment, but the obedient response we give to the greatness of God as He reveals Himself. Congregational song, regardless of style, is that opportunity of the people of God to respond to God in worship and adoration, surrender and praise. It is that expression that reflects the unity of the Body of Christ and is best done through the identity of common experience.

3. Is the melody of the tune really singable? At first, this may sound somewhat elementary, but in a day when a large portion of worship songs are taken from group or solo recordings, it is an important question to ask. Just because a group records a particular song does not automatically make it a viable option for the congregation. Some songs were designed to be "listened to," more than "sung with." These types of songs definitely have a place as a testimony to God's work in the life of the composer or even the singer, but are difficult for a group to sing. In evaluating whether the melody of a song is really singable, consider the following:

A. Many artists have large vocal ranges, singing higher notes with ease. Because of this their recordings are done in a range that is comfortable for them, not for the average vocally-untrained person in the pew. Some worship leaders take these songs directly from chord charts to use in worship without regard to the group for which they will be used, resulting in limited participation. If a song is too high or too low the majority of the congregation will not participate. When in doubt, the leader can make arrangements ahead of time to lower or adjust the key to make it more accessible for the congregation. It may be harder for the leader, but congregational singing is not primarily about the leader, it's about the majority of the body of Christ being able to express itself corporately.

B. Sometimes the rhythm and melodic line of the song is so much like recitative, or like spoken text, and almost defies everyone singing together. Soloists, or small groups may be able to sing it well, but only after hours of practice. In a large group the ability to understand the text vaporizes as frustration sets in because the participants have to work so hard trying to stay together. This type of song is difficult for the congregation, and may not be the best choice if the focus is facilitating congregational participation.

C. Good melodies are memorable; they have "hooks" that keep pulling the singers back into the song and have some sense of internal repetition that helps the ear in learning the melody. They have a recognizable structure. They have melodies that are sung in the hearts of the congregation during the week when no one else is around. Songs that change structure with each verse or line and unpredictable melodic jumps are much more difficult to learn.

Good melodies have a balance between predictability and creativity that make them easy to remember and leave the listener with a desire to remember them. The texts should cover theological themes found in Scripture and be presented in a way that is not trite or that does not demean the meaning of the Scripture. The wedding of strong texts and good melodies makes for the best congregational expressions.

4. Is the song of lasting character, or is it more of a temporal filler? Songs that are based on cultural fads or are "ear candy" are probably not the best choice as a vehicle for corporate worship. Many times these songs use words and phrases associated with passing trends, so when the phrase becomes dated, the song loses its effectiveness. The choices of music used in worship can be driven by personal taste rather than service design. Instead of asking, "What is the best and most appropriate song for this service and message from God's Word?" –we just look for ways of including our favorites. There is a temptation to get caught up in the "latest and greatest" syndrome, where only the newest songs are chosen for use. The problem is the congregation never sings the same song enough times over a long period of time (for a year of more) so that a canon of easily remembered songs teaching theological doctrine is established.

No song is ever pushed into long term memory for meditation and reflection.

A related point is song association. Some songs become associated with certain movements and take on a life of their own. While this may be a great help to congregational worship, a danger exists of using melodies or styles that are so associated with something or someone not biblical, and it becomes difficult to bypass the association.[13]

5. Can the congregation follow? When a song is new, the congregation must learn both new text and melody. Obviously the words may be on a screen or as printed text, but rarely do congregations have access to any written music. Even when hymnals were in use, the majority of the congregation really couldn't read the notes. This means the congregation is dependent on learning the melody from hearing it sung and played. In guitar-driven worship, the learning of the melody is limited to the ability of the singer to lead with the voice, since chordal accompaniments lack melodic support. A great aid in correcting this deficiency is to use the piano, keyboard, or organ, which can help carry the congregation's melodic line. The less familiar the song, the more important melodic support for the congregation is necessary. No doubt congregations can learn a new melody without melodic support, but it is more difficult.

Now What? Corporate worship is different than gathering a group of individuals together just to sing. Corporate worship is dependent on a group of believers focusing on the worship and adoration of Almighty God. Something very special happens when that group comes together to express praise as the Body of Christ. Effective corporate worship is not dependent on a set of steps that guarantee success. There are no magic buttons to press that result in the corporate focus on God and His nature and character. Corporate worship means that the Body of Christ is participating, whether it be singing, praying, giving, sharing testimonies, or reading Scripture aloud. If the congregation is not participating, it is not corporate worship.

As far as the leader is concerned, personal preparation is indispensable; leaders cannot take people where they have not been. Corporate preparation is indispensable; congregations don't flip a switch and transform into a body of worshipers without conscious action. While there are many things that can be done to facilitate corporate worship, one important factor is to make sure any music used in worship is "congregational." A wise worship leader is aware and continually evaluates each song of each service with these things in mind.

Worship Leader or Lead Worshiper?

Often when the phrase "worship leader" is used, an image of someone on stage with a guitar and microphone is the first thing that comes to mind. Consciously or unconsciously this image of a performer becomes a model in the mind of the worship leader and the congregation, and the value given to the work of leading the worship experience depends on how closely the worship leader meets the image in his own mind or in the minds of the congregation. I would like to refocus and rethink some issues that I pray will have life-changing implications. Just as a biblical understanding of worship can change how we approach a Sunday worship service, so a biblical understanding of what is pleasing to God can help remold our thinking about leading worship. Paul wrote to the Christians at Rome:

> *I plead and beg you by God's mercies, to present your-selves as a pure and holy sacrifice to God, which is the rational thing to do when you think of all that God has done. Don't allow the culture of this age to mold you into its way of thinking and reasoning, but allow God's Word and way transform how you think and*

act, for this is pleasing to God. (Rom. 12:1-2, my paraphrase)

Paul was writing to a group of believers who needed to know how to grow in their faith in the midst of a pagan culture that was cruel, carnal and careless. More perhaps than in any other time in recent history, the Church today needs to hear the Apostle's words. We need a change of character brought about through changing how we think. We live in a society that lusts for entertainment, self-gratification, and self-indulgence and has successfully projected its philosophy into the Church itself, and unfortunately, this influence has spread into some of the very leadership of Christ's body.

Satan has been so successful in this implementation because he uses partial truth. He promotes a pastoral leadership style that is "my way or the highway," taking the prophetic role of the pastor and divorcing it from the servant leader model that Jesus gave. He promotes those leading worship to model themselves after "other professional entertainers" that know how to manipulate the crowds for maximum response, rather than be the transparent bridge and facilitator that reveals only Jesus. Satan's model for leadership promotes ambition for power, prestige and the measuring of greatness as having the largest crowds at concerts and sales of recordings, and a "serve me" mentality, while Scripture teaches that greatness comes from serving others. Scripture presents the leadership model of Jesus as one who taught with authority and served the other disciples. Biblical worship leadership is not based on how excited the crowd gets, or how loud the music and singing are, but how transparently Jesus is seen and magnified. We also have no way of outwardly measuring the personal motivations of a leader, nor is it our responsibility. God is the one that judges. We can avoid the trap of only looking at these external indications and remember what God told Samuel when he wanted to anoint one of David's brothers as king: "The Lord does not look at the things people look at. People look at the outward appearance, but the Lord looks at the heart" (1 Samuel 16:7).

I praise God for many pastors and worship leaders who have not succumbed to the temptation to assume power and prestige come from position. True power comes from the Spirit of God living through the life and character of the worship leader. The power that leadership affords is not a power to do what we desire, but the power to do what is right, being what we should be and doing what we should do. Biblical leadership is not dependent on how many people "jump when we say 'frog,'" but how much of the very nature and character of Christ is evident in how we relate with one another. True prestige is being approved by God.

Over and over Paul encourages this development of character through the surrender of our will:

- ✝ In 1 Corinthians 13, though we are articulate in various languages, and know
  everything about everything, and do not relate to one another in the love of Christ,
  we are nothing.
- ✝ In 2 Corinthians 12, God tells Paul that in difficulty His grace is sufficient and that it is

not through our greatness, but weakness that God's power is revealed.

✞ In Galatians 4:19, Paul relates that he is like a mother in labor until "Christ is formed in you."

✞ In Ephesians 1:4, before the foundations of the world we were chosen to be holy and blameless in His sight.

✞ In Ephesians 2:8-10, we are saved by grace through faith for God's purposes.

✞ In Philippians 1:6, we understand that God's work in our character is a process that He himself is working in our lives.

✞ In Philippians 2:5-11, we are called to let the attitude that was in Christ be ours.

✞ In Philippians 4:8-10, Paul gives us the beginnings of how to reshape the pattern of our thoughts.

✞ In 1 Thessalonians 1:5-12, Paul reminds them that he didn't come trying to impress them with fancy words, but with love lived out for their benefit.

✞ In 1 Timothy 3, as Paul shares qualifications for church leaders, his emphasis is on their character; make no mistake, correct doctrine is important and Paul covers that throughout the letter, but sometimes we pass up the other, relegating it only to those times when we ordain a pastor or deacon. Godly character is required of leadership.

✞ In 2 Timothy 2:14-15, Paul urges the young leader not to argue about words, but to live in a way that is approved by God, both by what he does and says. In Titus, Paul links right doctrine with right living.

These truths are easy to pass over. Often our focus is on right doctrine, but Paul reminded us in I Corinthians 13 that right doctrine in and of itself is not enough. As leaders, God has called us to relate with people in a manner that we reflect His nature and character. Our words alone, without the reflection of Him, are empty.

As leaders we must be careful to avoid equating *knowledge* of God's Word with the *practice* of God's Word. Knowing we should respond in love is not the same as actually doing it. As we put Scriptural principles into real life, they will reflect the nature and character of Christ as we relate to one another. This process takes time and requires a constant willingness to allow God's Spirit to work on the rough edges of our lives, our thought patterns and personalities.

Just because we are in a position of leadership does not mean that we are always right. One example that reminds me of the transformation of character is the apostle John. As a young man following Christ, he was named one of the "Sons of Thunder," ready to call down disaster on anyone not in line with what they were doing. Jesus rebuked him and James, and continued showing them what He was all about and what was really important. By the end of John's life, he was known as the "disciple of love," as he admonished the Christians in his last 3 letters time and time again to "love one another." We do not know all the details of what happened between John being called the "Son of Thunder" and his transformation to being called the "disciple of love", but there are some elements we can identify. John observed Jesus, the Lord of the universe, live out his life as a servant leader. In addition, the road to the cross and resurrection left indelible marks on the young disciple that never left his memory, as well as his understanding of the depth of God's love. As his experiences of life grew in number, so did his sensitivity to the Holy Spirit's prompting for change and learning how to respond in love.

One of the leader's greatest dangers is the belief he or she has arrived at a point where change is not necessary. I have heard it countless times through the years in statements like: "that's just the way I am...", "that's just not me..." and "I tried that and it didn't work..." I have seen these individuals go from one place of service to the next, always blaming someone else for failures. Is it possible God led them to a difficult place to help smooth out some of the rough spots in their character? But rather than being willing to change, they just kept on running to the next place, convinced that somewhere else things would be better. God is more interested in our character development than our convenience, He is more committed to forming Christ's nature and character in our lives, than leading us to a place with "no problems." We dare not fall into the trap of "entitlement," where we tell God that after all we have given up to follow Him, He owes us a good place to serve; that after all the sacrifices our family has had to make, we deserve only the best. Such a line of reasoning is not from the Holy Spirit of God.

In the years that God has allowed me to minister, I have seen scores of promising leaders go down in the flames of their own pride and stubbornness. Many others just give up the ministry after having been burned too many times or burned out in the process. Still others in their carelessness, disregarded little lusts in their lives and home and families were destroyed. With all the love of Christ possible, with tears of grief over so many that have fallen by the way, I am asking, pleading for all of us to stop and take account. There should be regular periods of checkups in our lives as well as accountability to others. Each year there must be a deepening of the relationship as well as growing in our depth of knowledge. As long as we have clay feet, this will be a struggle, but a struggle well worth the effort. In this way we can become, as I read once, "Lead Worshipers," not just "Worship Leaders."

Six Key Questions for those that Lead Worship
1. Am I prepared?

• *Spiritually prepared*— confessed, forgiven, reconciled with others, in right standing with the Father, obedient to what He has commanded me to do?

• *Musically prepared*— the service planned in tandem with the sermon, music rehearsed and ready, not just hastily thrown together or limited to personal favorites or ones that we don't have to really work on to do.

• *Physically prepared*— adequate rest, healthy diet, consistent exercise, so we can be at our best and not just be running on 2 cylinders or half asleep.

• *Mentally prepared*— We must have a strong biblical understanding of what worship is and is not, and we must be constantly teaching and reminding each other what worship is.

2. Am I worshiping?

• It is so easy to get wrapped up in the details of leading music, directing praise bands or small groups and choirs, checking microphones, monitors and lights, that we lose the goal of what and why we do what we do.

3. Am I leading?

• If only a few people are really following, we must ask ourselves if we are really leading. If we are not taking the congregation along with us, we are walking alone. As "lead worshiper (better term than worship leader), we help facilitate congregational worship, not provide religious entertainment.

4. Am I growing or coasting?

• Once we reach a certain level of "expertise" (for lack of a better term) in worship leading, it is easy to stop learning, stretching, and digging deeper. We fall back into lazy habits and some even come to the point where they think they have "arrived," and just don't need to study, practice, etc., since they are now "successful" in the ministry. This is a very dangerous attitude and one in which Satan loves to entice leaders.

5. Am I teachable?

• Similar to the previous one, but relates more to attitude and response; typically shown through the inability to take advice, and the assuming their way is the best.

6. Do I love people?

• Some leaders are so wrapped up in the music or themselves they see people just as a means of getting what they want or want done. They fail to see the needs, relate to their hurts, and believe that being served is more important than serving others.

I realize there are probably many more, but this short list can go a long ways to help us lead as Christ as called us to lead for His honor and glory!

Worship and Entertainment

"The church that can't worship must be entertained. And men who can't lead a church to worship must provide the entertainment." -A. W. Tozer

As a worship leader, Tozer's words make me really stop and think. His quote could have been said this last week instead of 45 years ago, and made me want to explore what he said further. This exploration is done with fear and trembling, since Tozer was one of God's giants and I don't feel as if I could add anything to the power of his words. (I would encourage the reading of his *What Ever Happened to Worship* and *Worship the Missing Jewel* for some background.) Of the many discussions that could be made from Tozer's comment, I just would like to briefly focus on the "entertainment" aspect and do it in a Q & A type format.

Q: What so wrong about entertainment, anyway? I listen to the radio all the time and when I go to church, I want to hear my favorite songs there too. Couldn't it be both worship and entertainment?

A: The first thing we need to clarify is what is meant by the terms "worship" and "entertainment." For simplicity, let's define worship as *that obedient response to the revealed nature and character of God.* Remember in Isaiah's experience (Isaiah 6) God revealed Himself as Holy and the prophet saw himself as sinful, he confessed and was forgiven. He was then able to hear God's voice and responded in obedience, "Here am I, send me." The focus of biblical worship is always God and God alone; Scripture calls anything less than that idolatry.

Entertainment may be defined as "*An activity designed to give pleasure or relaxation to an audience, no matter whether the audience participates passively as in watching opera or a movie, or actively as in games; a show put on for the enjoyment or amusement of others.*"[14] In both the intent of those performing and of those in the audience, the implied focus is, "How much does it please me?" Success in entertainment is measured in how well the audience found the performance *personally* pleasing. By nature it's designed for that purpose. The central focus of worship is pleasing God. Personal likes and dislikes are laid aside as the worshiper seeks to focus on thanking God for what He has done and praising God for His nature and character. Entertainment and worship are polar opposites in relation to their focus and purpose.

In a consumer-driven culture, we are accustomed to having everything cater to our personal desires. However, rather than being salt and light and a reflection of biblical values in the culture around us, many Christians have allowed the attitude of "have it my way" infiltrate worship in the church. One might expect this from a believer new in the faith, much like a baby who is unaware of anything but his or her immediate needs. The tragedy occurs when the baby never moves beyond this point, – as a human being or as a worshiper– each day living as if the world revolves around "I want this," and "I only like that." Unfortunately, our culture certainly provides little encouragement toward more mature attitudes.

Confusion also exists between entertainment and inspiration. Look at this definition of "inspirational" and compare it to that of entertainment: "*(a) a divine influence or action on a person believed to qualify him or her to receive and communicate sacred revelation (b) the action or power of moving the intellect or emotions...*"[15] That which is inspirational can help move someone beyond selfish motives. It may or may not be spiritual in nature; as in the inspiration received watching the Olympics and the fruit of hard discipline and practice, and it may even motivate to be more diligent in exercise. Some music may inspire people toward a deeper relationship with God, *but the focus remains on the receiver.* A person being entertained with music might only want more entertainment for their own personal fulfillment. (Some may consider that inspiration is related to worship, since it might result in some kind of response, while others may debate it still would be too tied to personal feelings and not solely centered on God. That is a debate best saved for another time.) Suffice it to say that there is confusion between entertainment and inspiration and it seems wiser to err on the side of caution, and maintain that worship finds its center in and on God, His nature and character and what He has done.

As we look at these considerations, we also need to reflect on why we approach God in worship in the first place. If we worship God so that our needs are met, we are focusing on ourselves. However, when we really focus on God in worship, somehow in God's grace, He meets our needs; the focus is on Him, not my needs or desires. We aren't to pretend we haven't needs when we come in worship. God invites us to bring our needs to Him; it is part of the model prayer that Jesus taught: "give us this day our daily bread..." At the same time we must remember that in that same prayer Jesus begins with a recognition of God's nature (*hallowed or Holy is Your name*) and a complete submission to God's will and purpose: "*Your kingdom come, Your will be done on earth as it is in heaven.*" Even in the context of the Model prayer, it is a matter of priority. In worship, as in prayer, the priority of our focus must be on God.

Q: How do we measure what is entertainment or not? Is it dependent on style or tempo? Should we question motives of those leading? Can those that lead worship do it in such a way that it is worship for them, but received as entertainment, or led is such a way that it is entertainment, but received as worship?

A: Judging or trying to discern whether or not something is "entertainment" is problematic in at least two points: First, our responsibility in worship is to focus on God, not measure how pleasing it may or may not be to us personally. We are not to approach worship from the standpoint of entertainment in the first place. Secondly, if we are focusing on God's nature and character, we are not trying to judge motivations of those participating.

Those leading worship who approach the service as "just another gig" are clueless as to their responsibility. I believe there is less of a possibility of worship when using a model that is entertainment driven simply because the goal and focus of the performers would not be centered in God, and would not be driven and controlled by the Holy Spirit. I don't doubt that such a model might produce a myriad of emotions, but our measure of worship is adherence to biblical truth, not feelings, since the "heart is deceitful above all things" (Jer. 17:9). As to whether a group that has lead worship in truly biblical manner might be perceived as entertainment, I believe that it is certainly possible if those on the receiving end are ignorant of what worship is and unprepared for it.

Worship should not be defined in terms of emotional expression, though such expressions are sometimes a result. The danger arises when we begin to measure our worship experience in terms of an emotional response. Consider the following statement: "I don't think I really worshiped today, I only got to like a '5,' instead of the "10" I had last week." Although few might say this out loud, the number of worshipers that "church hop" from church to church seem to express this intent of finding worship that gives them an emotional response. Let's review again the definition of worship: *that obedient response to the revealed nature and character of God,* not some predetermined level of emotional response. However, worship is not the annihilation of our personal level of emotional response; reading through the Psalms confirms the myriad of emotional expressions David had in worship.

Q: How are we to deal with our emotions, then, in worship?
A: Consider this illustration: A father goes on several business trips a year and each time brings a gift for the children. After a while, the children would meet him at the door when he

returned, but they really didn't want to see him as much as to see what he might had brought them. Their focus has changed from their father to what might be given. If we are not careful, our worship can shift from waiting on "Daddy" to the "gift." Whether or not there is a gift of emotion, that should not become the measure of our worship or our focus.

The depth of our knowing Christ is related more to our experience with Him, than just our feelings of emotions. The broader and deeper our life experiences, the wider and more profound the depths God can take us to show us more of Himself. I get to know Him as "Comforter," when I experience sorrow. I learn to know Him as my "Refuge" when in storm; as my "Healer" in sickness, etc. I may know mentally He is my "Teacher and Guide," but when I am faced with a difficult decision to make or direction to take, as I trust in Him, I learn from experience who He is those areas. The true depth of our knowledge of Christ is much more profound than our feelings and helps us learn the multitude of facets of His nature and character.

The role of the worship leader is not one of providing great entertainment. Churches that demand such only reveal how bankrupt they are in their understanding of biblical worship. Leaders that succumb to the temptations of entertainment miss the joy of pleasing the One who really matters. May God keep us focused on His priorities and grant us the desire to remain grounded in a biblical understanding of worship.

What is "Ministering to the Lord?

The phrase that is sometimes heard among those leading worship is that we must come and "minister to the Lord," and since the word "minister" can bring to our minds the idea of "meeting needs," we need to think seriously what we are saying. This is particularly interesting since God is self-sufficient and needs nothing. To help us think about this subject, I've listed the more prominent passages that deal with ministering to the Lord as well as ministering before the Lord, which is similar. The goal here is not to provide commentary for each passage, but see the common elements that exist.

Old Testament References:

Psalm 101:6
My eyes will be on the faithful in the land, that they may dwell with me; the one whose walk is blameless will minister to me.

Isaiah 56:6
And foreigners who bind themselves to the LORD to minister to him, to love the name of the LORD, and to be his servants, all who keep the Sabbath without desecrating it and who hold fast to my covenant—

Judges 20:27-28
And the Israelites inquired of the LORD. (IN THOSE DAYS THE ARK OF THE COVENANT OF GOD was there, with Phinehas son of Eleazar, the son of Aaron, ministering before it.) They asked, "Shall we go up again to fight against the Benjamites, our fellow Israelites, or not?" The

LORD responded, "Go, for tomorrow I will give them into your hands."

1 Samuel 2:18
But Samuel was ministering before the LORD—a boy wearing a linen ephod.

1 Chronicles 16:1
(Ministering Before the Ark) They brought the ark of God and set it inside the tent that David had pitched for it, and they presented burnt offerings and fellowship offerings before God.

Jeremiah 33:21
then my covenant with David my servant—and my covenant with the Levites who are priests ministering before me—can be broken and David will no longer have a descendant to reign on his throne.

Numbers 18:2
Bring your fellow Levites from your ancestral tribe to join you and assist you when you and your sons minister before the tent of the covenant law.

1 Samuel 2:30
"Therefore the LORD, the God of Israel, declares: 'I promised that members of your family would minister before me forever.' But now the LORD declares: 'Far be it from me! Those who honor me I will honor, but those who despise me will be disdained.

1 Samuel 2:35
I will raise up for myself a faithful priest, who will do according to what is in my heart and mind. I will firmly establish his priestly house, and they will minister before my anointed one always.

1 Chronicles 15:2
Then David said, "No one but the Levites may carry the ark of God, because the LORD chose them to carry the ark of the LORD and to minister before him forever."

1 Chronicles 16:4
He appointed some of the Levites to minister before the ark of the LORD, to extol, thank, and praise the LORD, the God of Israel:

1 Chronicles 23:13
The sons of Amram: Aaron and Moses. Aaron was set apart, he and his descendants forever, to consecrate the most holy things, to offer sacrifices before the LORD, to minister before him and to pronounce blessings in his name forever.

2 Chronicles 29:11
My sons, do not be negligent now, for the LORD has chosen you to stand before him and serve him, to minister before him and to burn incense."

Jeremiah 33:22
I will make the descendants of David my servant and the Levites who minister before me as countless as the stars in the sky and as measureless as the sand on the seashore.'"

Ezekiel 40:46
and the room facing north is for the priests who guard the altar. These are the sons of Zadok, who are the only Levites who may draw near to the LORD to minister before him."

Ezekiel 43:19
You are to give a young bull as a sin offering to the Levitical priests of the family of Zadok, who come near to minister before me, declares the Sovereign LORD.

Ezekiel 44:15
"'But the Levitical priests, who are descendants of Zadok and who guarded my sanctuary when the Israelites went astray from me, are to come near to minister before me; they are to stand before me to offer sacrifices of fat and blood, declares the Sovereign LORD.

Ezekiel 44:16
They alone are to enter my sanctuary; they alone are to come near my table to minister before me and serve me as guards.

Ezekiel 45:4
It will be the sacred portion of the land for the priests, who minister in the sanctuary and who draw near to minister before the LORD. It will be a place for their houses as well as a holy place for the sanctuary.

Joel 1:9
Grain offerings and drink offerings are cut off
from the house of the LORD. The priests are in
mourning, those who minister before the LORD.

Joel 1:13
Put on sackcloth, you priests, and mourn; wail,
you who minister before the altar. Come, spend
the night in sackcloth, you who minister before
my God; for the grain offerings and drink offerings are withheld from the house of your God.

Joel 2:17
Let the priests, who minister before the LORD,
weep between the portico and the altar. Let them
say, "Spare your people, LORD. Do not make
your inheritance an object of scorn, a byword
among the nations. Why should they say among
the peoples, 'Where is their God?'"

There is an interesting addition in two passages in 1
Chronicles 16:4 and 1 Chronicles 25: 6-7. The first passage
were to lead the praising of God through music, while the
other describes their particular work was that of leading, being
"trained and skilled" in music.

Summary of Old Testament "Ministering before the Lord":

1. It was restricted to the priesthood.
2. It was tied to the carrying out of their responsi-
   bilties to offer sacrifices on behalf of
   themselves and the people.

3. It was done in recognition of who God was and what He had done for them.
4. It was done in obedience to what God had commanded.
5. It was tied to worship.

Summary of New Testament "Ministering before the Lord":

The passages related to "ministering to the Lord" in the New Testament are limited.

The Acts 13:2 passage ("While they were ministering to the Lord and fasting, the Holy Spirit said, "Set apart for Me Barnabas and Saul for the work to which I have called them." NASB) might equally be translated "while they were worshiping the Lord" (NIV, NLT, ESV).

There are few instances where Jesus is "ministered to:" the first is after the temptation account in the wilderness and he was ministered to by angels (Matthew 4:11). Another is Jesus being anointed in the house of Simon the leper by the adulterous woman (Matthew 26:6-13), and a general reference to the women that offered help to Jesus and the disciples (Matthew 27:55-56) and the anointing of the Lord's body after the crucifixion might be considered in this same light (Mark 16:1). With the possible exception of the adulterous woman, which might be considered worship as well as service, the instances revolve around meeting the physical needs of Christ. The motivation for doing so was no doubt out of love.

In the Apostle John's Revelation, the idea of ministering seems to center around a constant recognition of the character and nature of God, from the angelic beings that proclaim His holiness (Revelation 4:8-11), and His work of salvation, who in response bow down before the throne saying "Worthy is the Lamb who was slain" (Revelation 5:12-14).

General Summary and Conclusions:

The common thread seems to be an awesome recognition of the greatness and majesty of the character of God and the recognition of His gracious redemption of His people through His great acts. Ministering to God would then involve an obedient response to God's character and work, or how worship itself may be defined: "The obedience response to the revealed nature, character, and work of God." As we worship God then, we are ministering to Him. The more that we understand about *who* God is and *what* He has done, the more that we can allow Him to renew and remold our minds and our thinking, the more that we will be better able to minister or worship Him.

God needs nothing, so there is no need in Him that we might possibly meet, however God does have desires: He desires to have a relationship with us. He knows that the most satisfying relationship that meets our inmost needs is found in our recognition of who He is and our submission to the plan that He has for us. We can only come to that relationship through the confession of our sins and recognition of God's saving act of redemption through His Son, Jesus. We must come to realization of the absolute power and authority of God over everything, and begin the process of grasping the depth of His love for us in what He did through Christ in redemption.

Our submission and obedience are tied to our understanding of who God is and what He has done. As we live our lives allowing His love and work as our point of reference, we joyfully submit our wills and lives to the One who loved us enough to give His own life to reclaim us, rising from the dead, showing His power and authority over even death itself. We respond in obedience to His nature and work. We can do nothing less than worship Him.

Are there bleating sheep in your ministry?

In 1 Samuel 15, Scripture relates the story of Saul's failure to completely follow God's instructions to completely destroy the Amalekites and how he allows the men to take the spoils, allowing the king of the Amalekites to live. When questioned by Samuel the prophet of God why he disobeyed, Saul only attempts to justify his actions. By calling his partial obedience a completed task, refusing to admit any wrong doing on his part, and blaming others for what had happened, Saul fails the true test that God was giving. The test was not just a call for an elimination of an old enemy of the Hebrew people, but a test to see if Saul would wholeheartedly follow God's command. Saul failed in several areas:

> **First,** he failed to see that partial obedience is disobedience.

> **Second,** he confused the task to be done for the lesson to be learned. By only focusing on the goal of winning the battle, he never asked himself if God might have a higher purpose in the assignment.

Third, he allowed fear to motivate his actions, rather than faith, because he defined who he was by what he did more than who God had called him to be.

Let's briefly look at each one of these. I was reminded of this first issue while visiting with our daughter who was correcting our grandson. After not doing all of what his mother had asked him to do, I heard her give some instruction and complete her statements with the phrase, "partial obedience is disobedience." I was completely impressed, for this is a lesson that really must be learned from childhood. *In God's sight, partial obedience is disobedience.* This may seem cruel and cold at first, but look at it this way. Suppose that the surgeon who is about to operate on you asks the nurse, "Has the scalpel been sterilized?" and she replies, "Yes, all but this one tiny part." Would you want the surgeon to use it? Of course not, for regardless how small that "one tiny part" may be, there could be enough bacteria to kill the patient. If this is true in our physical world, in the spiritual realm only God can see what lingering "bacteria" is left by our partial obedience, and such sin separates us from open fellowship with the Father. In the case of Saul, God's commentary is tragic: *"I regret that I have made Saul king, because he has turned away from me and has not carried out my instructions"* (1 Sam. 15:11). Samuel was angry, and he cried out to the LORD all that night. (Notice that Saul's disobedience was a grief to Samuel, who had anointed him as king. Our failures rarely affect only ourselves.)

As finite creatures we are incapable of understanding the infinite mind and purposes of God. However, that does not

121

mean that God does not want or allow us to discern some of the purposes of His actions. The most obvious revealed purpose is why He sent His Son to redeem man, – *"for God so loved the world."* Other areas of God's actions and will may not be so clear. Sometimes what God has called us to do is not as important as the character quality He is developing in us in the process of doing it. I remember in the movie, "The Karate Kid," the older master tells his young apprentice to paint the fence, but in a very specific way. Later, he has him polish a car, again in a very specific manner. The confused teenager obliged, but did not understand and finally in frustration tells the man that he came for training in karate, not to paint fences. Then the master shows him that the motions he gave for painting the fence were actually a part of a specific defensive move in karate. The activity was painting a fence, but the lesson was detailed training in defense. *Saul had confused the task to be done with the lesson to be learned.*

After Saul had defeated the Amalekites, he proceeds to set up a monument to himself. This is revealing in that he (1) takes credit for what God had done, not realizing that God had only used Saul as the instrument of His will, and (2) Saul was defining who he was by what he had accomplished, not by his character. Understanding this is key to the conversation that followed with the prophet in 1 Samuel 15:13-34. Rather than cite the entire passage, I will refer to specific parts. When Samuel finds Saul, probably in front of the monument he had set up for himself, Saul greets him, saying, *"The LORD bless you! I have carried out the LORD's instructions"* (v. 13). The prophet does not mince words in his reply: *"What then is this bleating of sheep in my ears? What is this lowing of cattle that I hear?"* Samuel was saying, "Saul, if you had obeyed I wouldn't be hearing what I am hearing. The proof of your disobedience is all around you." Saul then tries to shift blame: *"The soldiers brought them from the Amalekites; they spared the best of the sheep and cattle to sacrifice to the LORD your God, but we totally destroyed the rest"* [v.15]. Saul did not understand that disobedience is disobedience, regardless when attempts are made to spiritualize it. *He could not own up to his own failure of responsibility to oversee the actions of his troops.*

Samuel does not allow for excuses or justifications, his reply is swift and clear:

"Enough!" Samuel said to Saul. "Let me tell you what the LORD said to me last night." God doesn't play our games of trying to justify our actions. Samuel again confronts Saul with the truth: *"Why did you not obey the LORD?"* Saul fails to see this as an opportunity of grace and forgiveness on God's part and again tries to defend his actions: *"But I did obey the LORD," Saul said. "I went on the mission the LORD assigned me. I completely destroyed the Amalekites and brought back Agag their king. The soldiers took sheep and cattle from the plunder, the best of what was devoted to God, in order to sacrifice them to the LORD your God at Gilgal"* [v.20-21]. Saul just does not get it. Only when judgment falls does Saul begin to reveal the truth. Samuel's response to Saul's excuses are words that we must take to heart if we are going to have effective ministries. Listen first to Samuel's response to Saul's rationalization of his sin:

"Does the LORD delight in burnt offerings and sacrifices
as much as in obeying the LORD?
To obey is better than sacrifice,
and to heed is better than the fat of rams.
For rebellion is like the sin of divination,
and arrogance like the evil of idolatry.
Because you have rejected the word of the LORD,
he has rejected you as king." (1 Sam. 15:22-23)

The tendency is try to explain away our sin, to use the rationalizations we have used to delude ourselves in a feeble attempt to justify our actions to God. When Saul refuses to respond to the grace of God and admit guilt, judgment falls. Saul's rebellion against God was like idolatry in that he had set himself up as his own authority, worshiping the image of himself for what he had done. Saul had even taken that mental image of himself and turned it into a physical monument for him to admire. However, now it was too late, his unrepentant attitude has been judged by God and with one quick word, God has rejected Saul as king. Disobedience, especially among the leaders God has placed in power, has serious consequences.

The tragedy of the situation continues to unfold: *"Then Saul said to Samuel, "I have sinned. I violated the LORD's command and your instructions. I was afraid of the men and so I gave in to them. Now I beg you, forgive my sin and come back with me, so that I may worship the LORD"* (v.24-25). When Saul finally admits he is wrong, it is too late. God has already chosen another leader, one whose heart would follow after His. With his confession he revealed the motivation of his action: fear. Since Saul understood who

124

he was only by what he did, that is, king and leader of the army, he feared doing anything that would reduce their numbers, thus, weakening his image and potential. He was not depending on God for his battles, but sheer numbers of men. So, when the men wanted to take the plunder from the battle, Saul did not have the courage to trust God, to set the standard of complete obedience based on God's command to destroy everything. In short, he failed to see that his worth was not based on the size of his army or the battles won, but on what God had called him to do and be. [This is clearly seen later in the battle when David kills Goliath.] The price he paid was very costly, for though he continued to reign as king, he did so without the blessing of God, and he grew more self-centered and suspicious until he finally committed suicide on the battlefield.

Let's return to the original question, *"Are there any bleating sheep in your ministry?"* Bleating sheep can be any area of our lives in which we settle for less than complete obedience, any time we confuse the task to be done for the lesson to be learned, and any time we allow fear to motivate our actions, rather than faith, defining who we are by what we do more than who God had called us to be.

Do We Always Have to Learn Lessons the Hard Way? What we can learn from the life of Saul [*Part 2*]

When I was about 13 or 14, I reached into oven to retrieve a cast iron skillet my mother had asked for to make some cornbread. I had already turned on the oven some time before, and without thinking grabbed the handle with the force I knew it would take to pick up the heavy cast iron. Unfortunately, I

125

forgot, or was not thinking about the fact that the skillet would be hot and proceeded to burn my hand. Obviously, a foolish thing to do, but I can assure you that I have never repeated that mistake.

We don't always have to learn the "hard way," but can learn from the mistakes of others so that we don't have to "burn our hands" with every task that we are called to accomplish. As I have been working through the lives of Saul and David in my personal Bible study time, the Spirit of God keeps bringing me back to some lessons that He wants me to learn by observing the failures in the leadership of Saul. I am deeply concerned that those who lead worship lead in such a way that glorifies God and the tragedies exemplified in the lives of so many in Scripture. I would like to add four more lessons we can learn by understanding the failure from Saul, Israel's first king.

1. Saul confused manipulation with leading by a positive example. After Saul is crowned king, he received the news that the Ammonites were going to attack Jabesh in Israel (1 Samuel 11). Notice Saul's response in verses 6-8:

> *"When Saul heard their words, the Spirit of God came powerfully upon him, and he burned with anger. He took a pair of oxen, cut them into pieces, and sent the pieces by messengers throughout Israel, proclaiming, 'This is what will be done to the oxen of anyone who does not follow Saul and Samuel.' Then the terror of the Lord fell on the people, and they came out together as one."*

Saul is filled with the Spirit of God, but rather than saying that the pagans were defying the Living God (as David has done with Goliath), or even just sending pieces of the oxen out to everyone, he added a threat. In this initial call to arms, the fear of God came on the people and they follow "Saul and Samuel." God used Saul to win the victory in spite of the method of his recruiting troops, not because of it. This fear was initially motivated by the fear of losing their own cattle. (Already God had touched the hearts of some men to follow Saul [1 Samuel 10:26], but in this case Saul doesn't see them as enough, and Scripture is silent as to how many early followers there were.) Saul's relationship with God seemed to be secondary in that it was through Samuel, not one based from a personal walk with God. Saul could not lead by example, he had to default to manipulation and fear. Unfortunately, there are very few signs that his leadership skills ever surpassed these methods.

Worship leadership that stoops to manipulation and threats to "lead and motivate" others only proves that it can do neither: lead nor motivate. Such behavior reflects only great gaps of character and immaturity in their relationship with Christ.

2. Saul confused winning a battle with winning the war. After Saul defeated the Ammonites, there was a shift in Saul's battle plans. Where at first he responded in a defensive manner, his next move was offensive in character. In 1 Samuel 13, Saul and Jonathan made an unprovoked attack on a Philistine outpost and incurred the wrath of the pagan army. Over confident in his own abilities as commanding general, Saul's initiative proves his undoing. As the armies of the Philistines began to amass, fear overwhelmed the Israelite army, and Saul's soldiers began to scatter. Tired of waiting on Samuel the prophet and God's direction, Saul offered the sacrifice himself. This breach of practice was not a mere desire to have God's blessing and thus couldn't wait, it was direct disobedience to God's command.

Following God's instructions was not an option, but an absolute necessity for the leader God chooses. One victory doesn't guarantee future victory, and such assumptions are foolish especially when done outside the direct command of God. One poor decision only leads to another.

3. He shifted his focus to from defending the people to defending his position. Saul continued making poor choices, even when God gave him another opportunity by bringing retribution on the Amalekites for what they had done to Israel in the past. Unfortunately, Saul caved into his own fear of the men, and showed his lack of leadership again by not being able to control his own soldiers, as mentioned in the previous study. Saul's focus began to shift from this point on looking for the one that God had chosen to replace him as king. On numerous occasions Saul attempted to kill David. The longer he was in power, the more effort he put in chasing down David to take his life.

When some leaders sense their position and power are being threatened, their focus changes from doing what needs to be done to self-preservation. God is the ultimate protector of our reputation. The One who placed the leadership in the position they are in is well able to protect them or remove them as He sees fit.

4. He confused the mercy and grace of God with the approval of God. Perhaps one of the most bewildering things of all in this biblical account is that God left Saul in power for 40 years. Saul's life was marked with a few great military victories and a series of tragic failures as a leader. The longer Saul stayed in power, the more he assumed everything he did was right. He became his own standard for right and wrong. He misunderstood the mercy and grace of God that allowed him countless times and opportunity to repent and respond correctly.

God had even anointed David as the new king, but David does not take any initiative to remove Saul, allowing God to do this on His timetable. [Speculation that David was too young and lacked experience might be a valid consideration, as well as the fact that God was building His character into David by allowing him to go through the years of hiding from Saul. David needed to learn that God was his fortress and shield when being chased, he needed learn to seek God in discouragement, etc. Some of the most endeared psalms were written during these years. These are only speculations; only God knows why He allowed Saul to be King for so many years.] Saul just never understood what God was trying to do in his life.

We must never confuse God's mercy and grace with His approval. Sometimes God blesses us to bring us to repentance; sometimes he disciplines us to bring us to repentance. Saul's life ended tragically, and ironically after a failed attempt at suicide, at the hands of an Amalekite. His great battle victories forgotten, Saul leaves a legacy of failures in character and leadership.

Do we always have to learn lessons the hard way? What is the "take away" from the life of Saul as a leader? We must learn from the mistakes of leaders like Saul to help us avoid repeating similar failures.

    -We must lead by positive example, above reproach, never manipulating or in unethical ways.

-We must not confuse one or two major victories and think we are invincible.

-We must focus on what God has called us to do, not on how to keep our power and position.

-We must never confuse God's mercy and grace with His approval.

A Brief History of Congregational Worship: Where Are We in Music and Worship?

Before I start this reflecting, I must share my indebtedness to Dr. Harry Eskew, whom I had the privilege of studying with in my doctoral work and for his "*Sing with Understanding*," which is my resource for the following. In terms of where we are in music and worship in our churches today, the following outline might serve as a map much like you would find in a shopping mall that reads "you are here." So where are we? I'm asking your permission to "hang in there" for an extended response.

The simplest way to see where we are is to start with imagining the "song of the church through the ages" as though it were a big river, birthed from the Old Testament Psalms, New Testament canticles surrounding the birth of Christ, and the Pauline fragments. As the river continued to run, other smaller streams began to enter, such as the Greek hymnody of the Early Church. For several hundred years their hymnody centered on the transcendence and awesomeness of God, mostly called "canons" (not in the musical sense, like a round, but more like a hymn), one of which by John of Damascus had 250 stanzas. As the Christianity grew, so grew centers of liturgical tradition, predominately Greek, in Constantinople and Alexandria, and Latin, predominately in Rome. The Roman rite soon dominated the rest, except for Constantinople.

During the Dark Ages after the fall of Rome, the church became the repository for all knowledge and the arts. The Arian heresy arose in the 4th and 5th centuries, claimed that Christ was not divine, and gained wide spread acceptance because their doctrinal principles were put to catchy melodies and became very popular. (One chorus had the phrase, "there was a time when he was not..." Ambrose of Milan (creator of the long meter 8888) added another feeder stream by writing hymns to combat the heresies, until the Church fathers met to deal with the situation. The result was to prohibit all singing from the congregation and leave it solely to the priests. (This virtually remained in place until 1963 and Vatican II.) During the following centuries the song of the church was restricted to the few, not the masses.

The growth of church music centered around chant and related melodies until 1517 and Martin Luther began the new wave of thought: the allowing of the congregation to sing and sing in a language they understood. He encouraged the use of hymns as well as Scriptural texts for worship. (The adage that he used "bar songs" is probably more due to a misunderstanding of German Bar Form, in which structure most of the melodies were written — AAB. Granted secular melodies were used, but not necessarily "bar songs.") The coldness of the liturgy was again challenged with the rise of pietism (17th-18th centuries) and the need for personal emotional expression in the hymns used in worship. Out of the developments came Bach

131

and the contributions he made in church music. Each one of these added tributaries to the ever-widening river.

Meanwhile back in England, the influence of Calvin in Geneva was dominate most likely due to the political ties of the monarchs as well as the theological issues involved. Unaccompanied unison psalm singing was the only music allowed in non-catholic services. Many of the tunes from the *Genevan Psalter* of 1563 were adapted and used in English Psalters for the next 100 years until a Baptist pastor named Benjamin Keach read where Jesus "sang a hymn" after the Lord's Supper. Supported by scriptural direction, he wrote a hymn for his church that was to be sung after communion. This started a major controversy between the General Baptist (psalms only) and Particular Baptists (hymns allowed), even though the former believed in general atonement and the later were Calvinistic. The controversy raged on until hymn singing eventually became part of both groups' traditions. Psalms and hymns joined the ranks of those streams adding themselves to the river of praise.

One person's hymn texts that played an important role in the general acceptance of hymn singing was Isaac Watts. The genius and simplicity of expression help spread acceptance across the board with most groups. Many other ministers followed his style of writing. Later the Wesleys added greater dimensions to hymnody through their over 6000 texts and the compilation of rousing Methodist's tunes. (And Can It Be, etc.) The Welch added a rich heritage of hymnody through folk-like melodies and John Newton (Anglican, yet very evangelistic) William Cowper produced their "*Olney Hymns*" in England.

Two substreams came as an outgrowth of the above, each contributing to the whole: the Evangelical Tradition (i.e. Havergal, "Take my life and let it be,") and the Churchly Stream and the rise of the Oxford movement, which was an attempt by the Anglican church to recapture the Greek and Latin hymns and a link to the past, since their abrupt birth after the King broke away from the Catholic church. One major product of this movement was the hymnal, *Hymns Ancient and Modern* (1861), in which specific texts were set for specific melodies for the first time.

At first, the United States had very little contributions of their own to the larger river; William Billings, being the first American composer. The development of American hymnody was dependent on several influences: psalmody, German chorale tunes, and the rise of American folk tunes. These folk tunes basically came for two sources, the shaped note tradition that evolved out of the Great Revivals of the 1840's and the Spirituals that came from the slave songs. Lowell Mason led the attempt to reform congregational song by following music that was "scientifically composed," that is that followed the European model, not that of the singing schools of the South.

It was during this last half of the 19th Century that there was a rise of denominationalism, each with its own traditions and each with its own contributions to the main stream of worship and praise. The rise of Gospel hymnody was due in large part to the birth of the Sunday School movement as well as the early revival teams, such as Moody-Sankey, who popularized the genre until it was common place. Though many of the songs were conceived for "revival use" and not for Sunday worship, they soon found their place in the larger stream. Gospel songs continued through the Stamps-Baxter quartets and more modern versions of music like the Gaithers.

In 1950's, an Anglican minister attempting to reach the youth of his day set the music of the Anglican service to the current musical style (which sounded much like music from the early Disney movies), but began what we know today as the contemporary worship movement. This was fed in large part to the Jesus' movement in the US in the 1970's, and continued to develop until the genre came into its own commercially in the 1980s and 1990's. Certainly an oversimplification, but this is only a tracing outline a best.

Throughout history, virtually in every case when an new stream entered the river, there was turmoil, confusion, and conflict, but eventually the new tributaries would leave their mark with only the more lasting contributions lasting in the larger stream. Conflict and controversy have been a part of the music and worship world from the beginning. It has never been easy and sometimes it has been very ugly.

So if we were to describe "where we are now," I would have to say that we are obviously in a little stream that is trying to mix with the larger river. To be able to navigate correctly we need to keep in mind some very important things:

1. The tributary is not the main stream, only a part of it. Much conflict arises when a group confuses its contribution as the whole, instead of just part. The larger stream is the one that will be around for the longest. We must look for those things that are of true lasting quality, rather than follow

the temptation of chasing passing fads. As long as we are standing in the tributary, what we see may not be the entire story, but only a part.

2. People will misunderstand. The tendency is to gravitate to the style that we personally like the best, however, this is to focus on the part and not the whole. We must help them see the larger picture of how it fits together in the context of worship.

    We have failed to teach where we come from. And so we are like the Israelites coming out of exile whose children had failed to learn Hebrew, we have grown up generations who have not know Joseph.

3. Many times the controversy surrounding a new stream that was entering was calmed when the quality of the new genre was raised to higher standards. (i.e. Watts' hymns help lay to rest the psalms/hymns controversy) The Getty/Townend material has been a great help in this regard, with deep theological text, without resorting to useless repetitions.

4. Biblical worship demands that we be inclusive, and not given to entitlement. Biblical worship demands that we center our focus on Christ and His work, not our preferences. Biblical worship is not entertainment driven.

5. I think we need to keep anchored in the river, not the various streams that may arise and not confuse one for the other.

Endnotes

1. Bob Kauflin, *Worship Matters: Leading Others to Encounter the Greatness of God.* (Wheaton, IL: Crossway Books, 2008) 97.

2. Timothy M. Pierce, *Enthroned on Our Praise: An Old Testament Theology of Worship,* (Broadman and Holman Academic: Nashville, 2008), 36.

3. All Scripture will be taken from the New International Version unless otherwise noted.

4. Hunter College Reading/Writing Center, http://rwc. hunter.cuny.edu/reading-writing/on-line/prep-def.html. (Accessed September 21, 2007).

5. Tremper Longman and David Garland, "Psalm 24," *Psalms; The Expositor's Bible Commentary,* Revised Edition, Volume 5, by (Zondervan: Grand Rapids, MI, 2008) 257-262.

6. There are some wonderful commentaries on these passages and much has been written and the reader is encouraged to plumb their depths. This study will not attempt to duplicate the material, but summarize major points.

7. Ellen Bass and Laura Davis, *The Courage to Heal* (New York: Harper and Row, 1988), 150.

8. For more on this read "When God Seems Silent and Our Worship is Dry" found at the *Worship HeartCries* blog: http://www.edsteeleworship.com/2010/11/when-god-seems-silent-and-our-worship.html

9. Mark Galli, *Christianity Today*, accessed April 2010, at: (http://www.christianitytoday.com/ct/2010/aprilweb-only/25-41.0.html)

10. Eric Benoy, in a personal email, 4/16/2010, used by permission.

11. Much of what is called "Emerging Worship" is geared to personal, rather than corporate experience.

12. Brian Wren, *Praying Twice: The Music and Words of Congregational Song* (Louisville, KY: Westminster John Knox Press, 2000), 225.

13. For example, for those that remember the television show "Gilligan's Island," the melody fits great with the text for

"Amazing Grace," but to use it with those individuals, almost always causes a grin, because in the minds they are thinking about the program as they sing the text.

14. Found at http://en.wiktionary.org/wiki/entertainment

15. Found at http://www.merriam-webster.com/dictionary/inspirational

General Selected Bibliography for Worship

Abernethy, Alexis D., ed. *Worship that Changes Lives: Multidisciplinary and Congregational Perspectives on Spiritual Transformation.* Grand Rapids, MI: Baker Academic, 2008.

Adams, Jere V., ed. *Handbook to The Baptist Hymnal.* Nashville, TN: Convention Press, 1992.

Allen, Ronald and Gordon Borror. *Worship: Rediscovering the Missing Jewel.* Portland, OR: Multnomah Press, 1982.

Allen, Ronald. *The Wonder of Worship.* Nashville, TN: Word Publishing, 2001.

Arn, Charles. *How to Start a New Service.* Grand Rapids MI: Baker Books, 1997.

Barry, James C. and Jack Gulledge. *Ideas for Effective Worship Services.* Nashville, TN: Convention Press, 1977.

Bartley, James W. *Worship That Pleases God: Biblical Perspectives.* Akure, Ondo State, Nigeria: Baal Hamon Publishers, 2008.

Basden, Paul A., ed. *Exploring the Worship Spectrum: 6 Views.* Grand Rapids, MI: Zondervan, 2004.

Bateman, Herbert W. ed. *Authentic Worship: Hearing Scripture's Voice, Applying Its Truths.* Grand Rapids, MI: Kregel Publications, 2002.

Beach, Nancy. *An Hour on Sunday: Creating Moments of Transformation and Wonder.* Grand Rapids, MI: Zondervan, 2004.

Begbie, Jeremy, ed. *Beholding the Glory: Incarnation through the Arts.* Grand Rapids MI: Baker Books, 2000.

_____. *Resounding Truth: Christian Wisdom in the World of Music.* Grand Rapids, MI: Baker Academics, 2000.

Berkeley, James D., ed. *Leadership Handbooks of Practical Theology.* Grand Rapids MI: Baker Book House, 1992. vol. 1: *Word and Worship.*

Bertrum, M.H. *Worship in the Name of Jesus.* St. Louis, MO: Concordia Publishing House, 1968.

Best, Harold M. *Music through the Eyes of Faith.* San Francisco: Harper, 1993.

Bloy, Myron B., Jr. *Multi-Media Worship: A Model and Nine Viewpoints.* New York: The Seabury Press, 1969.

Bowman, Clarice. *Restoring Worship.* Nashville: Abingdon-Cokesbury, 1951.

Boyer, Horace Clarence. *An Analysis of Black Church Music with Examples Drawn from Service in Rocheser,* New York, 1973

Buchanan, Colin Ogilvie. *Services for Wholeness and Healing: the Common Worship Orders.* Cambridge, England: Grove Books, 2000.

Bradshaw, Paul F. *The Search for the Origins of Christian Worship.* New York: Oxford University Press, 1992.

Brenner, Scott Francis. *The Way of Worship: A Study in Ecumenical Recovery.* New York: The Macmillan Company, 1944.

Brink, Emily R., ed. *Authentic Worship in a Changing Culture.* Grand Rapids MI: CRC Publications, 1997.

Burkhart, John E. *Worship: A Searching Examination of the Liturgical Experience*. Philadelphia, PA: The Westminster Press, 1982.

Call to Worship: Liturgy, Music, Preaching & the Arts. Louisville, KY.: Office of Theology & Worship, 2003.

Carroll, Joseph S. *How to Worship Jesus Christ*. Chicago, IL: Moody Press, 1984.

Carson, D. A. *Becoming Conversant with the Emerging Church: Understanding a Movement and its Implications*. Grand Rapids, MI: Zondervan, 2005.

_____. ed. *Worship: Adoration and Action*. Eugene, OR: Wipf and Stock Publishers, 2002.

Carson, Tim and Kathy Carson. *So You're Thinking About Contemporary Worship*. St. Louis, MO: Chalice Press, 1997.

Christensen, James L. *Contemporary Worship Services*. Old Tappan, NJ: Fleming H. Revell Company, 1952.

_____. *Creative Ways to Worship*. Old Tappan, NJ: Fleming H. Revell Company, 1966.

Corbitt, J. Nathan. *The Sound of the Harvest: Music's Mission in Church and Culture*. Grand Rapids MI: Baker Books, 1998.

Christensen, Tara Dawn. *Choirs vs. Praise Teams: a Historical and Descriptive Account of Worship Practices in Large Evangelical Protestant Churches in America,* 2002.

Clark, Linda J., Joanne Swenson, and Mark Stamm. *How We Seek God Together: Exploring Worship Style. http://baptist.nobts. edu/ipac20/ipac.jsp?session=126Q008H00364.244182&- profile=no&* Washington, D.C.: Alban Institute, 2001. 1 13 min. videocassette.

Davis, H. Grady. *Why we Worship.* Philadelphia: Muhlenberg Press, 1961.

Dawn, Marva J. *A Royal Waste of Time : the Splendor of Worshiping God and Being Church for the World.* Grand Rapids, MI: W.B. Eerdmans Pub., 1999.

_____. HowShall *We Worship? Biblcal Guidelines for the Worship` Wars.* Wheaton: Tyndale House Publishers, 2003.

_____. *Reaching Out without Dumbing Down: A Theology of Worship for This Urgent Time.* Grand Rapids: Eerdmans, 1995.

Doran, Carol and Thomas H. Traeger. *Open to Glory: Renewing Worship in the Congregation.* Valley Forge, NY: Judson Press, 1983.

Dyrness, William A. *A Primer of Christian Worship: Where We've Been, Where We Are, Where We Can Go.* Grand Rapids, MI; Cambridge, U.K.: William B. Eerdmans Publishing Company, 2009.

Eskew, Harry and Hugh T. McElrath. *Sing with Understanding.* Nashville, TN: Broadman, 1980.

Flynn, Leslie B. *Worship: Together We Celebrate.* Wheaton, IL: Victor Books, 1978.

Foster, Richard. *Prayer: Finding the Heart's True Home.* San Francisco, CA: Harper, 1992.

Frame, John M. *Contemporary Worship Music: A Biblical Defense.* Phillipsburg, NJ: P&R Publishing, 1997.

_____. *Worship in Spirit and Truth: A Refreshing Study of the Principles and Practice of Biblical Worship.* Phillipsburg, NJ: P&R Publishing, 1996.

Gaddy, Welton. *The Gift of Worship.* Nashville, TN: Broadman Press, 1992.

Gappa, Vincent A. *Worship in a Symbological World: Enhancing Christian Worship in an Electronic Culture 2001.*

Hardin, *Grady. The Leadership of Worship.* Nashville, TN: Abingdon, 1980.

Harland, Mike, ed. *The Baptist Hymnal.* Nashville, TN: Convention Press, 2008.

Harland, Mike and Stan Moser. *Seven Words of Worship: The Key to a Lifetime of Experiencing God.* Nashville: B & H Publishing Group, 2008.

Highfield, Ron. *Great is the Lord: Theology for the Praise of God.* Grand Rapids, MI; Cambridge, U.K.: William B. Eerdmans Publishing Company, 2008.

Hill, Andrew. *Enter His Courts with Praise! Old Testament Worship for the New Testament Church.* Grand Rapids MI: Baker Books, 1993.

Hipps, Shane. *The Hidden Power of Electronic Culture: How Media Shapes Faith, the Gospel, and Church.* El Cajon, CA: Youth Specialties, 2005.

Hurst Lynn. *Changing Your Tune!: the Musician's Handbook for Creating Contemporary Worship.* Nashville, TN : Abingdon Press, 1999.

Hurtado, Larry W. *At the Origins of Christian Worship: The Context and Character of Earliest Christian Devotion.* Grand Rapids MI: Eerdmans Publishing, 1999.

Hustad, Donald P. *Jubilate! Church Music in the Evangelical Tradition.* Carol Stream, IL: Hope Publishing Company, 1981.

Johnston, Robert K. *Reel Spirituality: Theology and Film in Dialogue.* Grand Rapids MI: Baker Books, 2000.

Jones, Cheslyn, Geoffrey Wainwright, and Edward Yarnald. *The Study of Liturgy.* New York: Oxford University Press, 1978.

Joyce, Derek and Mark Sorensen. *When Will Jesus be Enough? Reclaiming the Power of Worship.* Nashville, TN: Abingdon Press, 2008.

Kauflin, Bob. *Worship Matters: Leading Others to Encounter the Greatness of God.* Wheaton, IL: Crossway Books, 2008.

Kendall, R.T. *Before the Throne.* Nashville, TN: Broadman and Holman, 1993.

Kimball, Dan. *Emerging Worship: Creating Worship Gatherings for New Generations.* Grand Rapids, MI: Zondervan, 2004.

Liederbach, Mark and Alvin L. Reid. *The Convergent Church: Missional Worshipers in an Emerging Culture.* Grand Rapids, MI: Kregel Publications, 2008.

Leisch, Barry. *People in the Presence of God: Models and Directions for Worship.* Grand Rapids, MI: Zondervan.

_____. *The New Worship: Straight Talk on Music and the Church.* Grand Rapids MI: Baker,

Lucado, Max. *Come Together & Worship.* Nashville, TN: J. Countryman, 2003.

Lucarini, Dan. *Why I Left the Contemporary Christian Music Movement: Confessions of a Former Worship Leader.* Webster, NY: Evangelical Press, 2002.

Martin, Ralph P. *The Worship of God.* Grand Rapids MI: William B. Eerdman's Publishing Company, 1982.

_____. *Worship in the Early Church.* Grand Rapids MI: William B. Eerdman's Publishing Company, 1964.

Maxwell, William D. *A History of Christian Worship.* Grand Rapids MI: Baker Book House, 1936.

Maynard-Reid, Pedrito U. *Diverse Worship: African-American, Caribbean & Hispanic Perspectives.* Downers Grove, IL: Inter Varsity Press, 2000.

Miller, Kim. *Handbook for Multi-sensory Worship.* Nashville, TN: Abingdon Press, 1999.

_____. *Handbook for Multisensory Worship*. Vol. 2. Nashville, TN: Abingdon Press, 2001.

Mitchell, Robert H. *I Don't Like That Music*. Carol Stream, IL: Hope Publishing, 1993.

Myers, Robert A. *The Development of a Rubric for the Evaluation of Intimate Songs in Contemporary Christian Worship*. Theological Research Exchange Network, 2006.

Navarro, Kevin J. *The Complete Worship Leader.* Grand Rapids, MI: Baker, 2001.

_____. *The Complete Worship Service*. Grand Rapids, MI: Baker, 2005.

Noland, Rory. *The Heart of the Artist*. Grand Rapids, MI: Zondervan, 1999.

_____. *Thriving as an Artist in the Church*. Grand Rapids, MI: Zondervan, 2004

_____. *The Worshiping Artist: Equipping You and Your Ministry Team to Lead Others in Worship*. Grand Rapids, MI: Zondervan, 2007.

Peacock, Charlie. *At the Crossroads : An Insider's Look at the Past, Present, and Future of Contemporary Christian Music*. Nashville, TN: Broadman & Holman, 1999.

Parry, Robin. *Worshipping Trinity: Coming Back to the Heart of Worship.* Bletchley, Milton Keynes, UK; Waynesboro, GA: Paternoster Press, 2005.

Peterson, David. *Engaging With God: A Biblical Theology of Worship.* Downers Grove, IL: InterVarsity Press, 1992.

Phifer, Stephen R. *Worship that Pleases God: Loving God with Heart, Soul, Mind, and Strength.* Victoria, BC, Canada: Trafford Publishing, 2005.

Pierce, Timothy M. *Enthroned on Our Praise: An Old Testament Theology of Worship.* Nashville, TN: B & H Academic, 2008.

Pinson, J. Matthew, ed. *Perspectives on Christian Worship: 5 Views.* Nashville, TN: B & H Academic, 2009.

Ortland, Anne. *Up With Worship: How to Quit Playing Church* revised ed., Venture, CA: Regal Books, 1982.

Owens, Ron. *Return to Worship: A God-Centered Approach.* Nashville, TN: Broadman and Holman, 1999.

Pass, David B. *Music and the Church: A Theology of Church Music.* Nashville, TN: Broadman Press, 1989.

Ramshaw, Gail. *Christian Worship: 100,000 Sundays of Symbols and Rituals.* Minneapolis, MN: Fortress Press, 2009.

Rayburn, Robert G. *Oh, Come Let Us Worship.* Grand Rapids, MI: Baker Book House, 1980.

Redman, Robb. *The Great Worship Awakening: Singing a New Song in the Postmodern Church.* San Francisco, CA: Jossey-Bass, 2002.

Risi, Patrice. *Pop Goes the Worship : the Influence of Popular Music on Contemporary Christian Music in the Evangelical Church.,* 2007.

Rognlien, Bob. *Experiential Worship.* Colorado Springs, CO: NavPress, 2005.

Segler, Franklin M. and Randall Bradley. *Understanding, Preparing for, and Practicing Christian Worship.* Nashville, TN: Broadman and Holman, 1996.

Sharp, Avery T. and James Michael Floyd. *Church and Worship Music: An Annotated Bibliography of Contemporary Scholarship: A Research and Information Guide.* New York; London: Routledge, Taylor & Francis Group, 2005.

Shuttleworth, H.C. *The Place of Music in Public Worship.* London: Elliot Stock, 1892.

Siewart, Alison, ed. *Worship Team Handbook.* Downer's Grove, IL: InterVarsity Press, 1998.

Smith, Reginald. *Keep it Real: Starting a Christian Hip-hop Service in a Reformed Context.* Theological Research Exchange Network, 2004.

Smoak Jr., Alfred M. *Identifying Contemporary Praise & Worship Songs for Use During the Church Year at Trinity Baptist Church, Livermore, California.* Brentwood, TN: Worship Together, 1999.

The Worship Sourcebook. Grand Rapids, MI.: Calvin Institute of Christian Worship: Faith Alive Christian Resources : Baker Book House, 2004.

Towns, Elmer. *Putting an End to Worship Wars.* Nashville, TN: Broadman and Holman, 1997.

Towns, Elmer L. and Ed Stetzer. *Perimeters of Light: Biblical Boundaries for the Emerging Church.* Chicago : Moody Publishers, 2004.

Ward, Pete. *Selling Worship: How What We Sing has Changed the Church.* Ward Bletchley, U.K.; Waynesboro, GA: Paternoster Press, 2005.

Warden, Michael, ed. *Experience God in Worship.* Loveland, CO: Group, 2000.

Webber, Robert. *Signs of Wonder: The Phenomenon of Convergence in Modern Liturgical and Charismatic Churches.* Nashville, TN: Abbott Martyn, 1992.

_____. *Worship Old and New.* Grand Rapids, MI: Zondervan Publishing House, 1982.

Webber, Robert E. ed. *The Complete Library of Christian Worship.* Vol. 1-7. Nashville, TN: Star Song Publishing Group, 1994.

White, James Emery. *Opening the Front Door: Worship and Church Growth.* Nashville, TN: Convention Press, 1992.

White, James F. *Christian Worship in North America : a Retrospective.* Collegeville, MN: Liturgical Press, 1997.

_____. *Introduction to Christian Worship.* Nashville, TN: Abingdon Press, 1982.

White, James F. and Susan J. White. *Church Architecture: Building and Renovating for Christian Worship.* Nashville, TN: Abingdon Press, 1988.

White, Susan J. *Christian Worship and Technological Change.* Nashville, TN: Abingdon Press, 1994.

_____. *Foundations of Christian Worship.* Louisville, KY: Westminster John Knox Press, 2006.

Whitesel, Bob. *Inside the Organic Church: Learning from 12 Emerging Congregations.* Nashville, TN: Abingdon Press, 2006.

Wiersbe, Warren W. *Real Worship: It will Transform Your Life.* Nashville, TN: Oliver Nelson, 1986.

Williamson, Robert L. *Effective Public Prayer.* Nashville, TN: Broadman Press, 1960.

William, William H. and Robert L. Wilson. *Preaching and Worship in the Small Church.* Nashville, TN: Abingdon, 1980.

Willimon, William. *The Service of God: Christian Work and Worship.* Nashville, TN: Abingdon Press, 1983.

_____. *Worship as Pastoral Care.* Nashville, TN: Abingdon, 1979.

Wilson, Melva, consultant editor; Joseph E. Troutman, John C. Diamond, editors; Reta L. Bignam, assoc. editor. *African American Worship : Faith Looking Forward .* Atlanta, GA: Interdenominational Theological Center, The Journal of the Interdenominational Theological Center, v. 27, no. 1-2, 1999.

Wiseman, Karyn L. *Grace Space: The Creation of Worship Space for the Postmodern/ Emerging Church .* 2006.

Witvliet, John D., ed. *A Child Shall Lead : Children in Worship : a Sourcebook for Christian Educators, Musicians, and Clergy.* Garland, TX: Choristers Guild; Grand Rapids, MI: Calvin Institute of Christian Worship, 1999.

Woods, Robert and Brian Walrath, eds. *The Message in the Music: Studying Contemporary Praise and Worship.* Nashville, TN: Abingdon Press, 2007.

Worton, Roland. *Emerging Worship: Becoming Part of the Sound and Song of Heaven.* Shippensburg, PA: Destiny Image Pubs., Inc., 2008.

Wren, Brian. *Praying Twice: The Music and Words of Congregational Song.* Louisville, KY: Westminster John Knox Press, 2000.

Wright, Tim and Jan Wright, eds. *Contemporary Worship: A Sourcebook.* Nashville, TN: Abingdon Press, 1997.

York, Terry W. *America's Worship Wars.* Peabody, MA: Hendrickson Publishers, 2003.

York, Terry and C. David Bolin. *The Voice of Our Congregation: Seeking and Celebrating God's Song for Us.* Nashville, TN: Abingdon Press, 2005.

17548568R00093

Made in the USA
Middletown, DE
28 January 2015